THE TRUST EFFECT

people skills for professionals

The new business agenda of the '90s focuses on working with change and developing people's potential and performance. The *People Skills for Professionals* series brings this leading theme to life with a range of practical human resource guides for anyone who wants to get the best from their people in the world of the learning organization.

Other Titles in the Series

COACHING FOR PERFORMANCE
The New Edition of the Practical Guide
John Whitmore

CONSTRUCTIVE CONFLICT MANAGEMENT
Managing to Make a Difference
John Crawley

EMPOWERED!
A Practical Guide to Leadership in the
Liberated Organisation
Rob Brown and Margaret Brown

LEADING YOUR TEAM
How to Involve and Inspire Teams
Andrew Leigh and Michael Maynard

LEARNING TO LEAD
A Workbook On Becoming a Leader
Warren Bennis and Patricia Ward Beiderman

MANAGING TRANSITIONS
Making the Most of Change
William Bridges

NLP AT WORK
The Difference that Makes a Difference
in Business
Sue Knight

POSITIVE MANAGEMENT
Assertiveness for Managers
Paddy O'Brien

THE POWER OF INFLUENCE
Intensive Influencing Skills in Business
Tom E. Lambert

THE STRESS WORK BOOK
Second Edition
Eve Warren and Caroline Toll

THE TRUST
EFFECT

Creating the high trust,
high performance organization

Larry Reynolds

NICHOLAS BREALEY
PUBLISHING

LONDON

To Monica, Sorcha and Róisín

First published by
Nicholas Brealey Publishing Limited in 1997

36 John Street	17470 Sonoma Highway
London	Sonoma
WC1A 2AT, UK	California 95476, USA
Tel: +44 (0)171 430 0224	Tel: (707) 939 7570
Fax: +44 (0)171 404 8311	Fax: (707) 938 3515

http://www.nbrealey-books.com

Library of Congress Cataloging-in-Publication Data
Reynolds, Larry.
The trust effect : creating the high trust, high performance
organization / Larry Reynolds.
p.   cm. — (People skills for professionals)
Includes bibliographical references and index.
ISBN 1-85788-186-9 (p : alk. paper)
1. Organizational behavior.   2. Trust (Psychology)
3. Organizational effectiveness.   4. Employee activation.
5. Management — Employee participation.   6. Industrial productivity.
I. Title.   II. Series.
HD58.7.848 1837
658.3´14—DC21   97-33455
CIP

ISBN 1-85788-186-9

British Library Cataloguing in Publication Data
A catalogue record for this book is available from the British Library.

Printed in Great Britain by Biddles Ltd.

Contents

Acknowledgements

Many people contributed significant time and ideas to this book. I would especially like to thank: Bob Alexander, Presiley Baxendale, Sandra Burslem, John Carlisle, John Dwyer, Shona Falconer, Tessa Gordziejko, David Green, John Hambidge, Patrick Hare, Peter Hewitt, Cherry House, Brian Howard, Ian McDermott, Kevin Newman, Michael Parkinson, Mike Parsons, Stewart Pierce, Madi Pilgrim, Clive Rawson, Penny Sharland, John Stanley, Margaret Stewart, John Tarrant and Phil Ward.

Two people deserve special mention: Nick Brealey and Monica McCaffrey. My publisher Nick exemplifies high trust relationships at work. Unstinting in his criticism for the many inadequate ideas and drafts I set before him, his belief in the project sustained me throughout. Without Monica's example, inspiration and sheer hard work, this book would have been a shadow of its present form. To you both, many thanks.

Overture

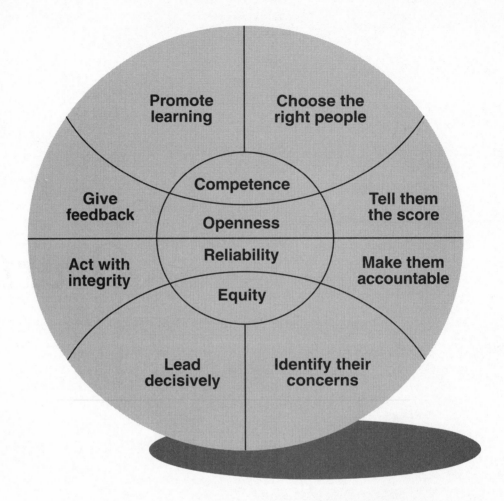

The Trust Effect

The Trust Effect 1

An Air Florida aircraft waits on the runway of National Airport, Washington DC, one winter evening. Conditions are bad. Despite the best efforts of the airport de-icing team, there are still icicles hanging from the wings of the aircraft. The co-pilot repeatedly draws the pilot's attention to this, but does so in a tentative manner – like many co-pilots, he does not want to appear to challenge his senior officer's judgement. Equally, the pilot evidently does not trust the judgement of his second-in-command.

The last words recorded on the black box flight recorder are those of the pilot, dismissing his co-pilot's comments about icicles. Shortly afterwards the plane attempts to take off, but ice on the wings causes it to crash into the Potomac river. All but 5 of the 74 people on board are killed. Their lives would have been saved if there had been more trust on the flight deck.

FORTUNATELY, few of us are directly involved in such dramatic situations. But running a business is every bit as demanding as flying a modern aeroplane, and the margins of error are often every bit as tight. Just as trust can literally be the difference between life and death on the aircraft flightdeck, so trust can be the difference between the survival and extinction of a business.

WHY YOU NEED TO UNDERSTAND TRUST NOW

In a less competitive world, trust was a 'nice to have' issue. If your company based its relationships on trust that was pleasant for the people involved, but it didn't make a difference to the company's survival. Plenty of businesses could get by with relationships based on power, if not on downright fear. In the new, intensely competitive world, trust is a '**must have**' issue. If you don't harness the trust effect to get results and drive down costs, someone else in your line of business will – and they will drive you out of business.

Partly in response to global competition, but partly because it is just fashion, the structure of organizations is changing too. Organizations are flatter and organize around processes rather than traditional departments. Teamwork is all the rage, as is outsourcing, the practice of contracting to suppliers or partners anything but the core business of the company. Power relationships just don't work for these new organizational arrangements. Trust-based relationships are the only viable option.

Destroying trust

The paradox which every CEO, team leader and employee needs to be concerned about is this: the forces which make trust more vital in the workplace are the same forces which destroy it. Let's just consider one response to global competition – downsizing. In the first three years of President Clinton's administration, AT&T and IBM each laid off 120,000 people, General Motors axed 100,000, Boeing 60,000 and Sears 50,000 as corporate America struggled out of the recession. From the perspective of short-term survival, this may in some cases have been the right thing to do, although the evidence for this view is far from convincing. What is certain is that downsizing results in a massive loss of trust, not only on the part of the employees who are 'let go', but also for those remaining.

New organizational arrangements have fractured the bonds of loyalty which made trust possible in the past. The new trust takes time to develop. A rise in outsourcing means less security, less face-to-face working contact; as we shall see, both essential ingredients of trust. According to futurologists Jim Taylor and Watts Wacker, trust is an increasingly scarce commodity:

> When no industry sector in America save telecommunications is trusted by more than half the populace, when only 8 percent of Americans say they trust advertising messages, when only 12 percent trust most public-interest messages from large corporations, when only a quarter of Americans say they generally believe what they hear on television news and talk shows, it should come as no surprise that a presumption of trust has disappeared from corporate, commercial and interpersonal communications as well.

The story in the UK is similar. A recent MORI poll found only 15 per cent of the British public trust multinational businesses to be honest and fair, while 25 per cent trust the newspapers. (The same survey found that 83 per cent trusted their doctor, so there is still time for the British health service to avoid the disaster which has befallen its US counterpart.) The general picture is this: **not only is trust the key issue for business, but business is trusted less than ever before**. That's why it is urgent for anyone involved in business to understand what trust is and how you build it.

TRUST IS ABOUT RELATIONSHIPS

Trust is one reflection of the way relationships are conducted between people in an organization. And it is the relationships between people, not the people themselves, which distinguish a great organization from a mediocre one. In fact relationships are more important than that – the quality of relationships can mean the difference between success and failure.

Relationships are so fundamental to business life that we often don't give them a second thought. We just know that some people are good to work with and some people aren't. If we give any thought at all to why this is, we usually express it in terms of the individuals involved – Mary is good to work with because she's very decisive, Pete is difficult to work with because he never makes up his mind. This kind of analysis misses the point: it takes two to tango. If you want to know what's working and what isn't, you need to focus your attention not just on the individuals, but also on the relationship.

POWER RELATIONSHIPS

Fundamentally, there are three different ways of conducting a relationship. The first of these is based on **power**. People do things not because they want to, but because they fear the consequences if they don't do them. Every time you sign a contract with someone, you are entering into a power relationship. Contracts are essentially documents which say that if party A does this, then party B will do that, and if one party reneges on the deal then this is what will happen. Many relationships between managers and their staff are similarly based on power.

Carrots and sticks

Power relationships are based on a succession of carrots and sticks. In a typical power relationship, doing a task will be accompanied by a series of rebukes and rewards at each stage. If the rebukes and sanctions outweigh the rewards, then the power relationship will be very oppressive. However, it doesn't have to be this way; people sometimes enter happily into power relationships, especially if they are built around contracts which offer a fair deal to both parties.

Getting things done

The best thing that can be said about power relationships is that they are reasonably effective at getting things done. If you sign a contract for something, chances are the contract will be delivered on. If a manager in a hierarchical organization tells staff to do something, chances are the staff will perform – up to a point at least. But power relationships rarely deliver the very highest levels of performance, even if they rely more on the carrot than the stick.

Research shows that people who expect to receive a reward for completing a task or doing that task successfully simply do not perform as well as those who expect no reward at all. And in power relationships which rely more on punishment than reward, the more oppressive they are, the more people will try to get even. At best, demotivated and untrusted employees do the bare minimum they need to get by; at worst, they may actually indulge in acts of sabotage to get their own back.

To take but one example, a disgruntled employee of Thorn UK felt that his employers were making him work unnecessarily long hours and difficult shifts. He got his own back simply by unplugging the cables at the back of Thorn's main computer, which processes orders from the company's high street stores. The cost to the company of rectifying the damage was £657,000.

The bad thing about power relationships is that they are very costly. If someone has to be constantly checking and monitoring people to make sure they keep to their side of the bargain, that takes up a lot of time and effort. In organizational terms, these transaction costs, as they are called, reduce competitiveness. And they can be very burdensome. John Whitney, director of the Deming Quality Center at Columbia University, estimates that in many organizations up to 50 per cent of all costs go on checking, monitoring and other non-value-adding work. When consulting firm Arthur D Little conducted a survey in a major American automaker they found that research engineers spent 65 per cent of their time on non-value-adding work – the bulk of which was attending management review meetings and other administrative work.

Think for a moment about your own situation. In a typical working day, how much time do you spend being

Reducing competitiveness

monitored and supervised – attending meetings, submitting reports, complying with the company bureaucracy? How much time do you spend checking and monitoring the work of your staff? How often do you get sucked into office politics? And how much time is left for you to do the real work – work which adds value to the final product or service? When they think about it in this way, many people find John Whitney's figure of 50 per cent too low.

Oppression

But the worst thing about power relationships is what they do to people. For many of a us, a large proportion of our waking lives is spent in the workplace. Do you really want to spend that time oppressing others, or feeling oppressed? Exerting power over people to get them to do things they don't really want to do? Having other people exert power to get you to do things you don't really want to do? This isn't good, and it doesn't do you any good. It shows that you are not able to trust people.

Studies have shown that people who are inherently mistrustful have a greater chance of contracting a fatal disease. In one study over a 25-year period, those who scored low on trust had a mortality rate more than six times those of the high trust group, with coronary heart disease featuring prominently.

THE FALSE HOPE OF EMPOWERMENT

Because power relationships are so unsatisfactory, organizations have looked around for alternatives. Using the 'either/or' thinking which is sadly so prevalent in business, some companies have done away with virtually all forms of control. If using power relationships to control people every minute of the day is such a bad thing, so the reasoning goes, then a company based on no control at all must be a good thing. Just start treating people like adults, remove the controls and restrictions, and everything will be wonderful. Sometimes known by the dreadful 1990s buzzword 'empowerment', this approach bases relationships not on power but on **hope**.

In the Greek myth of Pandora's box, Zeus's wife opens a box from which escape all the evils of humankind. Just as she is about to close the lid, she notices a small white grub in there. She opens the box again and lets it escape. The small white grub is hope. Some say that hope was allowed free to mitigate the effect of all the other evils; but others say that hope was the worst evil of all, allowing people's spirits to be raised only to be dashed.

Most organizations which have experienced hope-based relationships would agree with the latter conclusion. Every organization which has taken this naïve approach has been disappointed. The classic example is Barings Bank. A young trader called Nick Leeson ran Barings' futures operation in Singapore. He was not held accountable for what he did in any way – in fact the bank's directors in London just hoped that he would do a good job. He didn't, and his incompetence cost the bank £890 million.

Fortunately, there is a third way of conducting a relationship – based on **trust**. In a relationship of trust, people will do things for you not because they have to (as in the power relationship), not because they hope it will do them good in the end (as in the hope relationship), but because they genuinely want to. And why should someone want to do something for you? At one level, they want to because they are confident that you are concerned about them – you have their interests at heart. At another level, they want to simply because they identify closely with your values and beliefs.

TRUST

US retailer Nordstrom knows about trust. As Donald Petersen, former chairman of Ford and a committed Nordstrom customer, wrote:

> Nordstrom hammers home the underlying truth: you must make the decision to trust people as customers and employees.

Nordstrom certainly doesn't believe in power relationships – its employee handbook is one page long and merely says: 'Use your good judgement in all situations.' So how does Nordstrom get its employees to want to deliver the outstanding customer service for which the company is famous? Employees **trust** the company. They trust the company to have their interests at heart – for example because Nordstrom's sales staff are some of the highest earners in the business. But more than that, employees trust the company because they identify with the company's values and beliefs about customer service. This may seem hopelessly idealistic, but an increasing number of companies around the globe are finding it very profitable to achieve this desirable state of affairs.

Trust is tough

In a trust relationship, people do things because they want to. But what if they don't? Is there any control at all in a trust-based relationship? There certainly is, and this emphasis on **accountability** is one of the important ways in which trust-based relationships are different. In a power-based relationship controls are many and frequent. In a trust-based relationship there is only one sanction: if trust is broken, then the relationship ends. At high trust Nordstrom, for example, each salesperson has a target hourly rate of around $10 an hour. If staff fail to generate enough sales to earn the commission equivalent to that rate, then the first step is for them to receive some extra coaching from colleagues or their departmental manager. If that fails, then they lose their job. Working for Nordstrom isn't for everybody. Trust is tough.

Trust-based relationships are more effective than power-based relationships and, in the long term, cost less to maintain. And although they require more effort than hope-based relationships, they are infinitely better at getting results. While it is useful to think of power, hope and trust as three distinct types of relationships, the change from one to another can often be quite gradual. A power relationship based on a formal contract can emerge over time into a trust relationship as the two parties get to know each other. Equally, a relationship of trust can degenerate into a power relationship as each party realizes that its trust in the other is not justified. More dangerously, a power relationship can slip into a hope relationship, usually with poor consequences for both sides.

TRUST AT WORK

So much for relationships in the abstract. How does trust deliver lower costs and better results in the tough world of business relationships?

If any enterprise is going to be successful, there are four sets of relationships it has to get right:

● vertical relationships between managers and staff

● lateral relationships within and between teams and departments

● relationships with suppliers and other business partners

● relationships with customers.

Get any of these wrong and your enterprise can go belly up.

This way of looking at things is applicable to any size of enterprise, from huge multinationals to fledgling start-ups. It is equally applicable to the units within a company as it is to companies as a whole. You don't have to be a CEO to know how important this is. Within your team there are vertical and lateral relationships which you must attend to; your team also has suppliers and partners and customers, even though they might be on the same payroll as you are. How can trust make a difference to these relationships?

Which company is going to be more competitive – one which employs four people who work together enthusiastically and competently to deliver value to

TRUST AND VERTICAL RELATIONSHIPS

customers, or one which employs three people to deliver value to customers and one person to monitor and supervise the work of the other three? Systems for supervision and checking constitute a double whammy for reducing competitiveness – not only do such systems divert people and resources to the wrong places, but they are profoundly demotivating to the people who are left doing the real work.

Hewlett-Packard

Hewlett-Packard is a company which realizes the value of trust between managers and staff. While other companies in the sector have experienced their ups and downs – Apple and IBM being two notable examples – H-P has grown consistently, in size and profits, since it was founded by Dave Packard and Bill Hewlett in a garage in Palo Alto in 1939. It now employs around 100,000 people worldwide. At the heart of the company's success is an approach to management called the H-P Way. Essentially, the H-P Way is about relationships based on trust, not power. Dave Packard used to make the point with the following story:

> Once we promoted a man, a good worker, to be the manager of our machine shop. A few days later he came to see me. He said he was having a rough time managing and wanted me to come to the shop and tell his people that he was their boss. 'If I have to do that,' I said, 'you don't deserve to be their boss.'

Much has been written about H-P's enlightened employee practices – how it was one of the first companies to introduce employee stock ownership plans in the 1950s and so on. But focusing on these issues misses the point. H-P has been successful, not because it has been an enlightened or caring employer – plenty of other companies have done this and gone down the tubes – but because such practices help to reinforce a more important message, that the company trusts its staff:

> So going all the way back to the beginning of the company, Bill and I have placed great faith and trust in

H-P people. We expect them to be open and honest in their dealings with others, and we trust that they will readily accept responsibility.

Let's play devil's advocate for a moment. Did H-P's success come from trusting its staff, or has it been able to trust its staff because it has always been a successful company? To put this dilemma another way, can trust help to turn around a very *unsuccessful* company?

Dunlop

Dunlop was once one of the great names in British industry. In the post-war period, the company was making tyres not only for the burgeoning motor industry, but also for both civil and military aircraft. But by the mid-1980s it was in deep trouble, and its 3000-strong workforce was deeply demoralized. Virtually the only communication between management and workers was via the trade union, and the news was always bad – redundancies, cutbacks and wage freezes. In 1984, Michael Edwardes, who had a fierce reputation from British Leyland for asserting 'the manager's right to manage', was brought on to the board with a brief to hammer the company into shape. But it was too late. Now technically bankrupt, the company was taken over and passed into the hands of Sumitomo Rubber Industries. The new Japanese owners took a very different approach to management – they wanted relationships to be based on trust, not power. Now named SP Tyres, the company is thriving: output per employee is double what it was in the last days of Dunlop, waste is down over 50 per cent and turnover per employee up over 130 per cent. Trust works in a turnaround too.

Starbucks

Starbucks chain of coffee bars is another remarkable success story. Over a ten-year period, it has grown from six stores in Seattle to a business with over 1300 stores and 25,000 employees. All too often in the fast food industry relationships between management and staff are poor – certainly based more on the carrot and the stick than on any notions of trust. But Starbucks bucks the conventional wisdom – it has been successful precisely because relationships between managers and staff are based on trust not power. CEO Howard Schultz comments:

> If there's one thing I'm proudest of at Starbucks, it's the relationship of trust and confidence we've built with the people who work at the company. That's not just an empty phrase, as it is in so many companies. This attitude runs counter to conventional business wisdom. A company that is managed for the benefit only of its shareholders treats its employees as a line item, a cost to be contained. Executives who cut jobs aggressively are often rewarded with a temporary run up in their stock price. But in the long run, they are not only undermining morale but sacrificing the innovation, the entrepreneurial spirit and the heartfelt commitment of the very people who could elevate the company to greater heights.

TRUST AND LATERAL RELATIONSHIPS

Lateral business relationships exist not only within teams, but between them. UK-based National Vulcan is an engineering insurance company. Originally founded in Victorian times to provide insurance cover for exploding factory boilers, it now insures over 2.5 million items of industrial plant, ranging from car repairers to nuclear power stations. Until recently, issuing a new policy took about three months. The application had to pass through the hands of 30 people in 10 different departments. But during that three months, only three hours were actually spent on processing the application, and of that three hours only three minutes required human judgement, so the rest could be automated. After a little soul searching, the company reorganized itself. Instead of applications being passed from department to department, they are now handled by one team – and processed within 24 hours.

Many companies are finding the advantages of organizing their work along lateral processes, rather than by hierarchies and departments. Apart from the speed and economy of doing it this way, customers like to deal with a single point of contact in a company. It's frustrating to be told: 'Sorry. I can't deal with that, I'll have to put you through to ...' And happy customers lead to more profit.

Lateral relationships have many advantages – but they only work if there is trust. Because the hierarchy isn't there, you can't fall back on power relationships when the going gets tough. And it's no use basing lateral relationships on hope – if they are to work in the long term, they have to be based on trust.

That is, of course, precisely the reason that so many attempts at reorganizing processes laterally fail – the trust is not there to sustain them. A whole industry has sprung up around the idea of reorganizing processes laterally: it is called business process reengineering. The problem with BPR, as it is known to its friends, it that the very idea of massive reorganization (and the job redundancies which often seem to accompany BPR initiatives) are profoundly destructive of trust. And that's why James Champy, one of the founders of BPR, was moved to admit that most BPR initiatives do fail. They fail not because the principle of lateral based processes is incorrect, but because the practice of making them work fails if insufficient attention has been given to building or restoring trust.

Why reengineering often fails

National Vulcan was one of the organizations which got it right. The company put a lot of effort into building trust throughout the change, ranging from the symbolic to the practical. When staff called the new managing director Mr Sinfield or even sir, he responded by asking them to call him Ken. The new processes were designed not by senior managers or consultants, but by cross-functional teams which included staff from some of the most junior ranks of the company. This effort paid off – the company, which had lost some £5 million in the year before the change, broke even the year after and made £5 million the year after that.

TRUST AND SUPPLIERS

In 1990 General Motors employed 850,000 staff and produced 8 million cars. Toyota, with 65,000 workers, produced 4 million. How come that Toyota was not only streets ahead on quality and reliability, but was able to produce half the cars that GM did with only 5 per cent of the workforce? Part of the answer is greater levels of trust between the Japanese managers and staff, and within the staff – relationships of trust which make initiatives like quality circles possible. But most of the credit must go to the way in which Toyota worked with its suppliers. Toyota bought in some 70 per cent of its components and services, whereas GM did most of the manufacturing in house. In fact, Toyota that year employed some 300 people in its purchasing function. How many people did GM employ in its purchasing function – bearing in mind that it then made far less use of external suppliers? About 6000. Why the big difference? Because GM's relationships with suppliers were based on power: lengthy contracts, extensive quality control and so on. Toyota's relationships with its suppliers were based on trust.

Partnering

When a company wants to build a new factory, office or plant it calls in the building contractors. A contract is drawn up, haggled about and crawled over by each side's lawyers before the work begins. If things do not go according to plan – and this is inevitably the case – it's common for relationships to become antagonistic and costly, for both sides. Is there an alternative? The John Carlisle Partnerships, a UK consultancy firm, believes there is. By bringing representatives of the company and the building contractors together for a 'partnering' workshop, they are able to ensure that the relationship is based primarily on trust, not on power – with big benefits to both sides.

When Welsh Water was considering a £6.2 million modernization of its Chester waste water treatment works, it asked John Carlisle Partnerships to run a workshop to begin the process of building trust between Welsh Water and Amey, the principal contractor. By the end of the two-day workshop all 20 participants had committed themselves to a charter for working together in partnership. Welsh Water operations manager Laurence Wheeler said:

Because of the charter I have been sure that my site manager and his staff are able to work with the contractor without continually having to think about the procedural aspects of their actions.

Site supervision costs have been substantially reduced as a result and regular design and value engineering meetings have helped to contribute to significant savings. The work was completed in half the usual time. Amey site agent Sas Ghavami says:

Paperwork has been reduced to a minimum by the partnering approach. There is no confrontation and I have only a very thin paper file compared to all the paperwork often seen on contracts. The resident engineer has an equally small file. We all work from the same office and attitudes have been transformed. I have never experienced such a high degree of co-operation and willingness to discuss issues openly and help each other find solutions.

I have to admit that the biggest downside to partnering comes when you move onto another project where partnering principles are not practised.

In *Trusting the Team*, John Bennett and Sarah Jayes of the Centre for Strategic Studies in Construction at the University of Reading looked at relationships between contractors and their customers throughout the UK construction industry. They concluded that partnerships based on trust cost, on average, 1 per cent of the total project costs to initiate, but were responsible for overall cost savings of between 10 and 30 per cent. As John Carlisle, who has been an authority on partnering for 20 years, comments:

Co-operation between industrial users and sellers is a far more powerful strategy for making them both more profitable in the long term than any adversarial approach yet devised.

Financial backers

If relationships of trust between companies and their suppliers lead to big cost savings, relationships of trust between companies and their financial backers can be even more crucial. Until recently, investment guru Warren Buffet was the richest man in the world. (In 1996 he was overtaken by Microsoft boss Bill Gates.) With a net worth of some $15 billion he is richer than many countries. Buffet's fortune comes from investing in other companies. Before he invests in a company, he investigates it thoroughly and deliberately. He takes the time he needs to make sure it is a company he can trust. Once he has purchased shares in a company, he is extremely loath to sell. Buffet's investment strategy has been very successful for him, and for the companies in which he invests. In fact most companies would like their investors to have Buffet's commitment.

Numerous commentators, including British economist Will Hutton, have attributed much of British industry's problems to the short-termism of funders. Perhaps this is why some of the most innovative and successful small and medium-sized companies are family-owned concerns – they can afford to work on long-term relationships of trust without being driven by the need to produce short-term dividends for investors.

TRUST AND CUSTOMERS

When British retailer Marks & Spencer offered its customers completely new product lines such as wines, household furnishings and financial services, they were an immediate success. M&S had no particular expertise in these areas, and there were already plenty of other specialist wine merchants, furniture stores and financial services companies with excellent products on offer. So why did M&S do so well with these new lines? Because it is trusted by its customers to an extent which is unrivalled by any other British firm.

Loyalty

When your customers trust you they stay loyal. And if they stay loyal, they are worth a lot more to you. It's a great deal more economical to service an existing customer than it is to attract a new one. And a close relationship with a loyal customer makes it easy to offer the kinds of products and services the customer wants – so they spend more.

Leo Burnett is the largest advertising agency in the world, with 63 offices across the world and a turnover of £600 million. The firm enjoys the best paid staff and the lowest prices in the industry. What is its secret? In a notoriously fickle industry, on average only 2 per cent of Burnett's clients are lost to competitors each year. Loyal customers are immensely valuable to the company.

US insurance giant State Farm insures more than 20 per cent of households in the USA and, with a capital base of more than $20 billion, is worth more than General Motors. *Fortune* magazine has called it the financial services industry's most successful corporation. Its secret? Highly trusted staff and agents, low costs and a customer reputation which means that it loses less than 5 per cent of its customers each year, far less than the industry average.

Public sector

Although I have focused on the advantages of trust to private sector companies, the results hold just as true for the public sector. Unfortunately, in this case it is easier to find examples where an absence of trust drives cost up and effectiveness down. The classic example is the US healthcare sector. As the trust between patient and doctor declines, so the costs of litigation and medical insurance rocket – around 40 per cent of the entire US health spend goes on insurance and administration charges. This means that although the US spends over 13 per cent of its GNP on healthcare – double that of the UK or Japan – its infant mortality, generally taken to be a good indicator of the overall quality of healthcare, is worse than that of almost any other industrial nation.

GLOBAL COMPETITIVENESS

Different cultures put the accent on different areas when it comes to trust. When a group of American businesspeople meets a group of Japanese businesspeople their approaches to building working relationships will be different. Typically, the Japanese will be more interested in getting to know their American counterparts and starting to answer the question: can we trust these people? The Americans will be more interested in talking business, with a view to getting the contract drawn up and signed. For them, the trust is in the contract. The Japanese want a trust-based relationship from the outset; the Americans' initial desire is for a power relationship.

In his blockbuster *Trust: The Social Virtues and the Creation of Prosperity*, Francis Fukuyama argues that some national cultures are inherently more trusting than others. Some countries, like Japan and Germany, find it natural to build business relationships on trust. Others, like China and France, find it more difficult. This, he claims, means that those countries which are able to build trusting relationships have a global competitive advantage.

WHAT YOU NEED TO BUILD TRUST

If trust relationships are so superior to any other kind, why are they not more common? There are three responses to this conundrum.

Trust takes time

First, trust takes time to develop. It requires an up-front investment. Admittedly, this investment pays handsome dividends later on if trust is established, but the investment is still required – even if it turns out that trust is not going to be possible. For some people the dilemma is quite simply this: can you trust trust? Are you willing to put time and money into developing a relationship, trusting that it will justify your efforts?

When I asked Marks & Spencer's divisional director John Stanley why he thought M&S was such a high trust organization, he replied unhesitatingly:

The key is the length of time. We've been building up trust and reputation for over 100 years. We've had relationships with key suppliers which date back 70 years or more. Some of our employment policies which promote trust with staff date back 50 years. The most important thing we do as a business is to maintain and nurture that trust and reputation.

This isn't to say that you can only build a high trust organization over decades. As we shall see later in this book, it's possible to turn a low trust organization into a high trust one in a much shorter time. There are exceptional circumstances in which trust can develop very rapidly indeed. If there is one extremely clear shared goal, and shared penalties for failing to achieve it, then it is possible to develop trust very fast. Members of the armed forces experience very high levels of trust when facing the enemy – in a sense, they don't have any option. In a business setting, task groups and project teams can sometimes develop high levels of trust very quickly in the face of a big challenge.

But this kind of trust is very brittle – it usually fails to persist beyond the immediate challenge. It's a bit like a holiday romance – it all seemed very real and intense at the time, but the feelings somehow don't transfer to another context. Incidentally, that's why many attempts at 'teambuilding' fail. It's very easy to get people to trust each other if you take them away from their normal work and give them a big challenge, but this new-found level of trust often doesn't last when the team is back at work.

The second requirement of trust is a measure of toughness. For all their posturing, low trust organizations are often remarkably tolerant of poor performance. Curiously, they often seem especially tolerant of poor performance towards the top of the hierarchy. High trust organizations go to great lengths to make it possible for everyone to achieve high standards, but if in the final analysis an individual does not contribute, the high trust organization will act quickly and robustly to remove that person from their position.

Trust has to be tough

The third reason that not all relationships are based on trust is the same reason that not all athletes go on to win Olympic medals – it takes a lot of skill, practice and sheer willpower to get it right.

Trust must be practised

That's where this book comes in. It will enable you to develop both the skills and the mindset you need to build high trust relationships at work.

Chapter 2 looks at the principles which lie behind high trust relationships and at the ingredients of the trust effect, which combine to develop and sustain high trust relationships. The remainder of the book considers each of these ingredients in turn and offers practical suggestions for putting them into practice in your organization.

YOUR OWN TRUST TEST

The way you relate to other people – how far you trust them – is the most important aspect of your working life. Before continuing to read this book, take a few moments to think about how you relate to other people right now.

Below are eight sets of statements. In each set, tick the one which best describes your current approach.

SET 1

A I know straight away whether a new person will fit into our team or not.

B I'm happy to work with pretty much anybody.

C I am very choosy indeed about the people I do and do not want to work with.

SET 2

A Part of my job as a manager is to protect my staff from all the masses of information they wouldn't understand and in any case don't need to know.

B As a manager, I tell my staff everything.

C I ensure that my staff know all about the purpose and values of our business.

A If you want a job done properly, do it yourself.

B I'm a firm believer in empowerment – if you simply take away petty restrictions in the workplace you can be sure that people will do a good job.

C I will ask someone to do something only if I am confident that they have the skills and commitment to do it well – and I've assessed the consequences of failure.

A The only way to make sure that people do a good job is to monitor them closely.

B Most people are trustworthy – they just need to be given a chance.

C I hold people accountable for their results, but I don't interfere with their methods.

A I don't have much time to listen to the concerns of my staff, unless it's something really serious.

B My staff don't need me to look after them – they are all responsible adults.

C Taking the time to listen to my staff and their concerns is very important.

A I'm not that keen on too much consultation – decisions made by committee are rarely the best ones.

B Democratic decision making is always best.

C The extent to which I consult with others depends on the nature of the decision.

SET 7

A Being ethical is all very well in theory, but in business you sometimes have to cut corners.

B You have to trust people to be guided by their own conscience when facing tricky issues.

C I strive to work to the highest ethical standards.

SET 8

A If someone messes up, I'll come down on them like a ton of bricks.

B If someone makes a mistake, it's generally best to give them another chance.

C I have a reputation for being fair, but very tough on those who do not produce results.

With the caveat that this is just your own impressions of yourself at this moment, what can you learn from this short exercise?

Mainly As

If you've ticked mainly As, then you are not particularly keen on trusting others at work. This attitude may have served you well in the past, but it will let you down badly in the future. Once upon a time, most workplaces were organized on the assumption that people were not to be trusted. But as we have seen, times are changing. This book will help prepare you to deal with these changes.

Mainly Bs

If you've ticked mainly Bs, you're likely to think of yourself as being quite a trusting kind of person. The trouble is, you are probably too trusting. Organizations which trust people without good reason don't survive for very long. This book will help you to trust people in a way that gets results.

Mainly Cs

If you've ticked mainly Cs, you are already working to some of the principles in this book – although you may not realize it. The book will help you understand why what you are doing works, so that you can do it even better.

Putting Trust to Work 2

ALTHOUGH the word trust is to be heard with increasing frequency in the world of business, it is rare to find any analysis of what actually makes a trusting relationship. Four principles underpin a relationship of trust:

- **C**ompetence

- **O**penness

- **R**eliability

- **E**quity

These four principles are at the CORE of the trust effect.

THE CORE PRINCIPLES

Competence is the ability to do a job well. I spoke with Sandra Burslem when she was about to take over as vice chancellor at Manchester Metropolitan University, with responsibility for 3500 staff and 30,000 students. I asked

Competence

her how she would engender the trust not only of staff and students but of all the university's other partners.

> You've got to earn trust. People must believe that you are competent – that you exercise sound judgement, that you are a safe pair of hands.

Let's say you are watching a climbing instructor leading a group of people up a crag. Do you trust her enough to clip on to her rope and let her lead you up the rockface? You will only do this if you believe that she is competent, not only to make the climb herself, but to guide you up it too. As we will see throughout this book, high trust organizations make sure that they work only with people who are competent. They also promote a climate of learning to make sure that even as circumstances change, those people remain competent.

Openness

Sandra Burslem's second response to my question about trust was in terms of **openness**:

> You have to be open with people. As transparent as possible. You have to take people into your confidence.

What a telling phrase that is. Taking people into your confidence means being open, honest and truthful with people. It means acting with integrity. Organizations can be pretty secretive places. In one Dilbert cartoon, the conversation between a manager and a staff member goes like this:

> Manager: Here's the company vision and business plan.

> Employee: 'Vision: empowered employees working towards a common plan.' Sounds good. But the business plan is blank.

> Manager: It's confidential.

Employee: How am I supposed to know what to do?

Manager: I'll yell at you if you do the wrong thing.

Unfortunately, too many organizations resemble the world of Dilbert. When people in organizations don't know the truth, they'll make it up – and what they make up is generally far worse than the reality. High trust organizations ensure that their people get to know the truth: the truth about the business as a whole and how it is doing (no confidential business plans) and the truth about individual performance.

Being competent and open is not enough. You have to do what you say you are going to do. People will only trust you if you are **reliable**, dependable and consistent.

Reliability

Some time after his release from 27 years' imprisonment, Nelson Mandela travelled to Cuba to appear at a rally with Fidel Castro. Politically, Mandela knew that it was unwise – at a time when he was building relationships between the new South Africa and Western democracies, it could do no good to be seen supporting a discredited dictator. But he went to fulfil a promise. In the very beginning, when Mandela was in jail and forgotten by most of the world, Castro had stood up for him and kept reminding the world of what was happening. Mandela had promised in return to support Castro, and he went to Cuba simply to keep that promise.

High trust organizations understand that reliability is an essential component of getting customers to trust them, so much so that some companies – Federal Express, Mercedes-Benz, Starbucks – have built their entire reputation on the basis of their reliability. They also understand that to be reliable you not only have to keep your promises, but you have to make people accountable for their actions. Both can be tough.

The final principle at the CORE of the trust effect is **equity**. Of course people are concerned about the outcome of any business transaction. From the trust perspective, what bothers them more is whether the

Equity

transaction has been conducted equitably and fairly.

Consider the case of Ontario-based Algoma Steel. In May 1991 the company's owner, Dofasco, then Canada's biggest steelmaker, decided that it could no longer sustain Algoma's mounting losses and $752 million worth of debt. It proposed slashing the workforce of 7000 by half and imposing an across-the-board pay cut. Unsurprisingly, the plan was completely unacceptable to the workers and put an end to any residue of trust that the workforce had in the management of Dofasco. Yet less than a year later, more than 85 per cent of the workers voted for a 15 per cent wage cut and a reduction in headcount of 1600 (albeit over a five-year period). What accounted for this change of heart? In the interim, Leo Gerard, head of the United Steelworkers Union of Canada, had masterminded an employee buyout. Among other things, he had hired top management consultants, corporate lawyers and investment bankers to teach the workforce how to run their own mill. By educating Algoma's workers and actively involving them in the decision, Gerard was able to save the plant, and probably the town of Algoma too. The final decision was almost as tough as the management's original proposal, but what had changed was the way it had been reached. Employees had been involved in the decision-making process, and were therefore confident that justice had been done. Within two years Algoma had become one of North America's most profitable steel mills, with a net income of $110 million and stocks worth $10 a share – a big increase on the 5 cent valuation at the time of the employee buyout.

Chan Kim and Renee Mauborgne, two academics at European business school INSEAD, quizzed 3500 managers about the subject of trust. They concluded that the only sure way to create a climate of trust in the workplace was to ensure that decisions were carried out equitably and fairly. But equity is a balancing act – what appears fair to one person may appear unfair to another. That's why high trust organizations don't assume that they know what's best for people – they take the time and trouble to find out what really concerns their customers, employees, suppliers and business partners. And then they act decisively on what they find.

These CORE principles – competence, openness, reliability and equity – are at the heart of the trust effect. If you want to build a high trust organization, you can put these principles to work in relationships between managers and staff, between departments and teams, with your suppliers and with your customers. They are especially relevant to building high trust teams. Is the team competent – does it know what it is in business for and does it have the skills it needs? Is the team open and honest in its communication, or are there secrets and cliques? Is it reliable – are team members able and willing to keep their promises? Is it equitable – are the workloads and the rewards shared out fairly between team members? The team will become a high trust team only when these issues are addressed.

Most people know that trust relationships are based on principled behaviour. But simply knowing that the principles are competence, openness, reliability and equity is not enough. You have to put the principles into practice.

There are two aspects of a trust relationship: you have to be able to trust them, and they have to be able to trust you. As you can see from the model in Figure 1, there are eight practices linked to the CORE principles. Let's begin with the four practices which will enable you to trust others with confidence.

- Competence: choose the right people

- Openness: tell them the score

- Reliability: make them accountable

- Equity: identify their concerns.

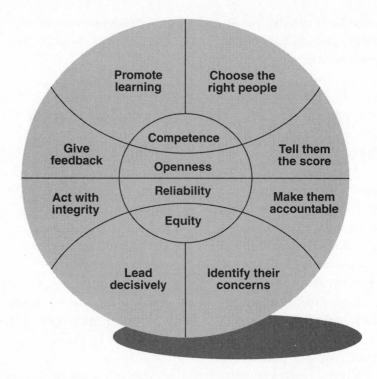

Figure 1   The trust effect

CHOOSE THE RIGHT PEOPLE

Not everyone has the potential to be competent in every circumstance. You might trust someone to do some baby-sitting for you, but not trust them to prepare your business accounts – or vice versa. Trust depends very much on the context. For this reason, high trust organizations don't just welcome in anybody, they choose the people who are going to be trustworthy in the context of that particular business. Low trust organizations often look for the wrong things and use the wrong process to assess them. One survey rates British interviewers as only 3 per cent more likely to choose the right person than if they were picking names out of a hat. High trust organizations put a great deal of time and effort into making sure that they have exactly the right person for the job – whether as employee, supplier or business partner.

As well as welcoming the right people in, high trust organizations are ruthless about getting the wrong people

out. If people are not competent to do the job, then the
organization cannot deliver reliably to its customers –
putting its entire reputation for trust in jeopardy.

Imagine that you are on an expedition through difficult
terrain. Each day you are told exactly how many miles you
need to cover, and precisely what scientific experiments
need to be conducted. The expedition is well equipped
and well resourced. The only thing is, you don't know what
it's for, where it's going and how well it's progressing. When
you ask the expedition leader, he says: 'I can't tell you
that, it's confidential – and even if I did tell you, you
probably wouldn't understand.' What would that do for
your motivation? What would that do for your trust in the
expedition leader? There can be no trust without
openness and honesty.

TELL THEM THE SCORE

   Most organizations operate like the expedition in that
example – they don't let people know how well the
company is progressing in achieving its overall purpose.
While it is common for organizations to have a mission
statement, this only tells you where the company would
like to be – it says nothing about how it is progressing
towards achievement of this goal. High trust organizations
are very open with people about the progress they are
making – they tell people the score.

In an organization based on power relationships, people
are constantly monitored and checked. Apart from being a
very costly way to run a business and profoundly
demotivating, this approach tends to blur the difference
between the important and the trivial. People can find that
they suffer more if they are late to work than if they fail
to perform in the job. But a company which values
compliance to its rules more than getting results is going
to find it hard to deliver reliably to its customers. That is
why in high trust organizations the focus is on results. If
you want people to be reliable and dependable, you have
to make sure that they have the resources to do the job –
and then hold them accountable for the results.

MAKE THEM
ACCOUNTABLE

IDENTIFY THEIR CONCERNS

If you are going to trust someone to do something, you have to be confident that they will want to do it. They are only going to have this confidence if they believe that you will deal with them equitably and fairly. The problem is that what may seem equitable to you may not appear equitable to them. Assumptions in this area can be highly dangerous.

When German automaker Volkswagen negotiated a 20 per cent pay *increase* with its workers in its Pueblo, Mexico plant, it assumed that this would be equitable recompense for some small changes in working practice that had been imposed. It was wrong – the workers saw the changes in practice as grossly unfair, and they would not be bribed into accepting them. A strike cost the company over $300 million.

The only way to ensure equity in relationships is to find out what the other party really wants. That's why in high trust organizations, chief executives spend a lot of their time doing just that – they get out and about to listen to the concerns of their employees, customers, suppliers and business partners.

BEING TRUSTWORTHY

Trusting others is only half of the story. Do the others trust you? Here are the four things you need to do to develop your trustworthiness:

- Equity: lead decisively

- Reliability: act with integrity

- Openness: give feedback

- Competence: promote learning.

LEAD DECISIVELY

If you want people to think that you conduct your relationships in a way that is equitable and fair, they will judge you by your actions, not your words. Listening to people is not enough: you must act. One of the most important class of actions on which people at work are judged is the way they make decisions. VW chose the wrong path in Mexico because it made the decision in the wrong way – it assumed that negotiating with union leaders was enough and that it didn't need to communicate with workers directly. Knowing the right way to make a decision so that the decision is seen to be equitable is an essential skill for any high trust relationship.

Just imagine what it would be like if you could rely on other people to keep their promises. If the builder who said 'I'll be there on Tuesday and finish the job by the end of the week' really kept this promise. If a colleague who said 'I'll find out and ring you back straight away' really did that. If the person who said 'You'll get the cheque tomorrow' honoured that commitment. Wouldn't the world be a much better place? What a great competitive advantage this would give to any person, team or organization which operated in this way. And integrity is not just a question of keeping promises – it also means acting to the highest ethical standards.

ACT WITH INTEGRITY

If you want people to believe that you are really open and honest, sharing any old information isn't enough. You have to tell them what you think of them – or, to be more precise, you have to tell them what you think of their behaviour. Such straight talking is rare in many organizations. In some cultures it is considered uncouth, or even unacceptable. Many people would like to be more open, but fear that too much openness may actually harm a relationship. High trust organizations know that the opposite is the case. Giving honest feedback enhances the quality of a trust-based relationship – provided that it is done well.

GIVE FEEDBACK

Being competent is no guarantee of staying competent in a rapidly changing world. The only way to stay competent is to make a commitment to learning. That's why high trust organizations don't just commit themselves to traditional forms of learning like training courses. They are fanatical

PROMOTE LEARNING

about finding opportunities every day for everyone involved in the enterprise to learn and develop. In *Built to Last*, Jerry Porras and James Collins identify the characteristics of American companies which have continued to be successful year in year out. Unsurprisingly, one of the key factors is a commitment to continually learning how to do things better.

From the trust perspective, a fast way to determine the level of trust in a company or team is to ask any of its members how well it is doing. If you're told that everything is fine you should smell a rat; but if you hear that things are going pretty well but they could be doing better, the chances are that the levels of trust will be high.

BEING COMMITTED

Take a look at Table 1 and see how different levels of trust result from different levels of commitment to the eight practices. How does your company measure up?

Table 1   Are you a high trust organization?

Practice	Low trust	Medium trust	High trust
1. Choose the right people	A very slapdash and hurried approach to recruitment	Conventional recruitment of staff – maybe a couple of one-hour interviews	A very thorough process which involves at least 12 hours' contact with successful candidate before appointment
2. Tell them the score	Mission statement – if any – regarded with cynicism	If asked, everyone would give a similar reply to the question 'What is this organization for?'	Everyone able to explain how the company as a whole measures success
3. Make them accountable	A lot of blaming others	People have to get permission from their bosses to do things	When something needs to be done, someone does it, knowing that the organization will support them

Practice	Low trust	Medium trust	High trust
4. Identify their concerns	Chief executive never seen	Chief executive has an open-door policy	Chief executive frequently out and about, talking and listening
5. Lead decisively	Staff dissatisfied with the way most decisions are made	Complaints that the managers 'never listen to us' when making decisions	All staff understand how important decisions are reached
6. Act with integrity	Sloppiness. A promise counts for little. Hypocrisy. Bending the rules	Only a little progress chasing. Meetings start within 10 minutes of advertised time	Every promise kept. Meetings start and finish on time. People act consistently and ethically
7. Give feedback	Lots of talking behind people's backs. Lots of 'office politics'	A company appraisal system which most people find useful	People get frequent feedback from everyone they work with
8. Promote learning	Not much training or development	Quite a bit of training and development	A big commitment to training and development

INFLUENCES ON GOOD PRACTICE

Just because you know what you should be doing to create a high trust organization doesn't mean that you are actually able to do it. Three influences determine whether we can in fact practise any behaviour:

- skills

- environment

- beliefs.

SKILLS

The remainder of this book is devoted to each of the eight practices which make up the trust effect. In each chapter, we'll look at the skills which you need. For example, when it comes to choosing the right person, you need the skill of knowing what you want from another person, the skill of designing an appropriate process to select such a person, and the skill of perceptive listening so that you can use this process to find the right person – someone you can trust.

Of course, simply reading this book won't give you the skills – you also have to practise them. To get really good at any skill you have to practise it, the more the better. But practice alone isn't enough – you have to have some way of finding out whether you are actually getting any better. Otherwise you are like the manager who once came on one of my training courses. He'd been sent by his company, but so far as he was concerned he had nothing to learn. In fact, he said to me at the beginning of the course: 'There's nothing you can teach me about management – I've got 40 years' experience of managing a coal mine.' As the course developed, he became aware that he hadn't had 40 years' experience – he'd had one year's experience repeated 40 times over. So as you begin to apply some of the ideas in this book, make sure that you have some way of knowing whether they are working for you. In some cases it will be obvious to you, and in others it won't. If you're not sure ask for feedback – from someone you trust.

ENVIRONMENT

Have you ever had the experience of learning a whole new raft of skills on a training course and then being unable to use them back at work? Even if you have the skills, you can only practise them if the working environment is right. By working environment I mean all the external influences on our behaviour – other people, the physical environment, the organization's systems and structures.

Systems and structures

Do the systems and structures in your organization have an effect on the levels of trust? You bet they do! In

1970, social psychologist Philip Zimbardo created a simulated prison in the basement of the Psychology Department at Stanford University. He filled it with the most normal people he could select, students who had completed a series of psychological tests. At the flip of a coin, students were randomly assigned the roles of prisoners and guards. The experiment was designed to last for two weeks. Zimbardo wrote:

> At the end of only six days we had to close down our mock prison because what we saw was frightening. We were horrified because we saw some boys ('guards') treat the other boys as if they were despicable animals, taking pleasure in cruelty, while other boys ('prisoners') became servile, dehumanized robots who thought only of escape, of their individual survival and of their mounting hatred of the guards.

Whatever else this experiment demonstrates, it confirms something that many people who work in organizations instinctively know – its structures and systems have a profound effect on the behaviour of the people who work there. The wrong kind of systems and structures lower trust and can even force them to do things which are clearly in no one's interest. When Bell Telephone instructed its operators to end *every* customer interaction with 'have a nice day', it created a great deal of discomfort for the operators who were receiving emergency calls. When you've just called an ambulance to attend to a severely injured daughter, it's not so great to be told 'have a nice day'.

Organizational systems are rarely neutral as far as trust is concerned. If an organization has a good performance appraisal system, it will encourage feedback and promote trust. If an organization has a poor appraisal system, it will hinder communication and destroy trust. As we examine each of the eight practices, we'll be looking at the kinds of systems and structures which best promote them.

Unless you are a chief executive or personnel director, you may feel that you have little influence on your

Other people

organization's systems and structures. As I was once asked: 'How can I develop a high trust team when I am saddled with a performance appraisal system which forces me to rank my team members one against another?' Systems and structures do have an impact on trust, but they are only one of the external influences on behaviour. Arguably, the strongest external influence is the behaviour of other people; and so far as your team is concerned, you have a great deal of influence. In particular, you can influence your own behaviour. We've already seen how reliability – also known as dependability or consistency – is a key principle of trust. Nowhere does this apply more in the consistency between what you are saying and what you are doing. If you want to create a high trust team, talking about trust won't do it. You have to demonstrate it every day, every minute in fact, with your actions.

Physical environment

Finally, a brief word about the physical environment. It's no coincidence that virtually all of the high trust organizations discussed in this book prefer the physical layout of their offices and factories to be open plan and single status. In some of them the chief executive not only eats in the same canteen as everyone else, but he or she works in the same open-plan workspace as everyone else. High trust organizations work hard to deliver a consistent and reliable message about the way they want to conduct relationships at work.

BELIEFS

A colleague of mine who is a consultant did a piece of work with a senior manager in a financial institution. The manager was known to be somewhat of an ogre and in his department trust, morale and productivity were all low. My colleague worked with him a little and introduced him to many of the practices in this book. The manager agreed that for one month's trial, he would work in a different way – essentially he would base his relationships on trust, not on power. During the course of the month, the department changed dramatically for the better, and in particular productivity hit an all-time high. But when my colleague returned to encourage the manager to keep up the good work, he got a nasty shock. Despite the success of the experiment, the manager had decided to go back to his old way of working. 'It's hard to put the reason into words,' he told my colleague, 'but deep down, I guess I just don't trust people.'

Whatever skills we have, however supportive the working environment, we will only do something if we believe that we should. Beliefs are the least understood but the most important influence on our behaviour. There are two very interesting aspects of beliefs. One is that people may be unaware that they hold a belief, even though it has a big impact on their behaviour. The manager at the financial institution in the example above didn't realize the extent to which he fundamentally distrusted people until he had a particular experience which brought it to his notice. The other interesting thing about beliefs is that they don't have to be, in any objective sense, true. Most of us hold some beliefs for which there is a great deal of supporting evidence and others which are frankly far fetched. We let both kinds rule our lives.

Let's take a look at some of the beliefs which might get in the way of practising trusting and trustworthy behaviour:

- We haven't got the time to choose the right people

- You can't easily measure progress in our business

- People cannot be trusted

- I haven't got the time to find out what everyone expects of me

- You can't please all of the people all of the time

- My work is too unpredictable to keep every promise

- If you tell people the truth it will demotivate them

- You can't teach an old dog new tricks.

If you are in the business of building relationships based on trust, then you need to have some awareness of your own beliefs in this area, and be open to change if they turn out to be counterproductive. Is it possible to change beliefs? Of course, otherwise you'd believe the same things now as you did when you were a child. How do you change beliefs? There are many ways, and here are three of the most useful approaches.

Take the belief to its logical conclusion

Take the belief to its logical conclusion. Let's take the belief that people aren't to be trusted. If you took that belief to its logical conclusion, what would that be like? Everyday life would be extremely difficult – you'd never eat a meal in a restaurant, you'd never travel in a vehicle driven by someone else, in fact you'd find driving yourself pretty stressful too, because you'd always be worried that other road users would swerve into you at any time. As for running an organization based on this belief, it would be like a labour camp. It would also be very inefficient. If taking a belief to a logical conclusion creates some feeling of discomfort, then it is going to be easier for that person to change to a new belief. It's a bit like the embarrassment some children feel when their schoolmates ridicule them for believing in Santa Claus. They're ready to take on a new belief.

Give counter examples

A second way of changing beliefs is to give counter examples. In the UK drinks market, Guinness was once widely believed to be a cheap drink for old men. This belief was a problem for the brand, because its customers were literally coming to the end of their drinking careers. Guinness repositioned itself by mounting a number of campaigns and promotions which repeatedly pictured Guinness as a drink for younger people. Today the brand is thriving. That's why this book – in common with many good management books – is full of case studies. It's a way of challenging a belief held by some readers to the effect that 'this is all fine and dandy in theory, but can it work in practice?'

Try on a new belief

A third way of changing beliefs is temporarily to suspend your old belief and try on a new one. Knowing that you can go back to the old belief makes it safe to try the new one. That's why organizations which pilot new ideas before implementing them are often more successful than those which go for the 'big bang' approach to change – it gives people a chance to try out some new beliefs without too much risk. When people temporarily suspend an old belief they may discover that the new belief is more likely to get them what they want than the old one.

As you read this book, you'll probably find that some of your beliefs are being affirmed and some of them challenged. Get curious about this. Ask yourself what kind of beliefs will help you to be trusting and to be trusted.

In the Overture we've set the scene for the trust effect: what it is, why it is such a good idea and, in general terms, how to achieve it. Now's the time to roll up our sleeves and get into the nitty gritty.

The Trust Effect

Choose the Right People   3

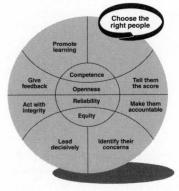

*C*HOOSING the right people to join a high trust organization is not easy. In a very short period – perhaps only a few hours – you need to make a decision about a working relationship which may last for years. In a low trust organization where people are constantly monitored and checked, an effective recruitment process is not so vital – all that really matters is a basic aptitude for the job. But in a high trust organization, you want to be able to trust people to get on with the task, with the confidence that they will do so not just well, but superbly. Not everyone has what it takes to thrive in such a working environment, so choosing the right person becomes a critical task.

In this chapter we'll look at the skills you need to be able to choose the right person. We'll consider these skills initially in the context of choosing employees, and then go on to see how they apply to choosing suppliers and other business partners. But the general approach is applicable to initiating any business relationship based on trust. We'll conclude the chapter by looking at the kind of tough decisions you might need to face when a working relationship has to come to an end, in other words when you have to fire someone.

HOW TO CHOOSE THE RIGHT PEOPLE

You need three skills to be able to choose the right person. You must be able to:

- be very clear about what you want from the person

- design an effective process to identify whether candidates have what you want

- listen perceptively.

Let's consider each in turn.

KNOW WHAT YOU WANT

A useful structure for defining what you are looking for in a potential employee is to think in terms of technical skills, people skills and values.

TECHNICAL SKILLS

Technical skills are the easiest to define. Examples are wordprocessing skills, knowledge of finance and accounting. How do you know that someone has them? They may well have formal qualifications, or you can ask them to talk about their experience. It is also possible to set up tasks to enable the person to demonstrate those skills there and then – you can sit someone at a computer and ask them to wordprocess a document or analyse a set of accounts.

PEOPLE SKILLS

Examples of **people skills** are the ability to work in a team, the ability to make decisions, creativity and flexibility. In high trust organizations, people skills are paramount. Technical skills, while important, can be taught and in any case tend to become out of date very quickly, so even if you choose someone who has that knowledge now, without a commitment to learning they will soon lose it. But people skills take much longer to learn. You want to choose people who are competent in their technical area – but you also want people who have the ability to be open, reliable and equitable.

How do you know that someone has people skills? Qualifications are of limited use here. A skilful interviewer can elicit evidence of such skills. The most reliable method is to set up some kind of practical activity which enables the candidate to demonstrate them.

VALUES

In the words of the song: it ain't what you do it's the way that you do it. Our **values** form part of our belief system, and, as we saw in the previous chapter, our beliefs have a big influence on our behaviour. High trust organizations value competence, openness, reliability and equity. They may make these values more specific – for example Nordstrom expresses its belief in reliability in terms of customer service, and Johnson & Johnson expresses its belief in equity in terms of its credo.

If you are going to be able to trust someone, you need to be clear what your organization's core values are (of which more in the next chapter) and then make sure that you choose people who are committed to the same values. How do you do this? Take the notion of customer service. A candidate may say that she believes in it. If you set up some kind of practical activity as part of the selection process she may demonstrate that she is able to give it. But does she have a long-term commitment to customer service which will last years into her employment? The only way to find out is to design a very thorough selection process which gets beyond superficial responses to reach a deeper understanding of what people really value.

WHAT TO LOOK FOR

Northern Foods employs over 20,000 people in food and dairy businesses throughout the UK. Because of the decentralized nature of the company and the high degree of trust given to each independent business, recruiting the right staff is crucial. What does group personnel executive Phil Ward want when recruiting a new managing director for one of Northern's companies?

We take great care in recruitment. Top of the list is a preference for the verbal over the written – we're looking for people who will work with their colleagues face to face, not send memos and reports. We also want people who can get on with it, develop others and get the best out of a team.

Telephone bank First Direct is one of the fastest growing businesses in the UK, attracting some 12,500 customers a month. Trust is a crucial factor in the bank's success. Customers must trust the bank to handle their financial transactions, even though they may never meet any of the bank's staff face to face and even though there is little of the written confirmation which accompanies even the simplest transaction at a conventional bank. So what does the company look for in its banking representatives? Commercial director Peter Simpson explains:

We take a lot of care with the people we bring into the business. We do not focus on the kind of education or formal qualifications that people have, their technical skills; these things can be trained. What we want to know is this: do they have the predisposition to the type of culture we have? Can they live our values as their own personal values?

DESIGN A PROCESS TO GET WHAT YOU WANT

Until the 1950s dock labourers in British ports were hired on a daily basis. Men available for work would meet at the appointed place and wave their union membership cards in the air. The foreman simply pointed at the men he wanted, choosing the most muscular and avoiding known 'troublemakers'. It was a degrading system, but in a rough and ready way it worked. The only skills then required of a dock labourer were strength and stamina.

In a curious way, recruitment practices in many organizations today aren't very different. Candidates meet at the appointed place, clutching copies of their CVs. They are herded one by one into an interview room to determine whether they have the skills for the job. In a very short time – perhaps an hour or so – it is all over.

High trust organizations are different. They know that a single interview is insufficient to determine whether someone has the technical and people skills and the values to join the organization and be trusted. So what do they do?

High trust organizations do include face-to-face interviews as part of their selection process. Taken together with any written information the candidate has provided – application forms, resumés and so on – these can provide a lot of useful information to help you find the right person. But there are two main drawbacks. First, the interview gives you information about what the person says, not what they do. Secondly, the interviewer needs to be pretty skilled at interviewing if he or she is going to extract useful information.

INTERVIEWS

For these reasons, high trust organizations always include some kind of practical test as part of their selection process. Giving someone an opportunity to demonstrate a skill is more reliable than merely asking them whether they have it. Practical tests can take many forms:

PRACTICAL TESTS

- Complete a written test

- Wordprocess a document

- Analyse a set of accounts

- Comment on a business plan

- Make a presentation

- Lead a group discussion.

Sometimes a number of practical tests are combined: in a

simulation of a busy morning at the office, a candidate may be asked to draft replies to a memo, analyse the key points in a report, respond to phone calls and even deal with difficult members of staff. This kind of test, which involves role playing, is often referred to as an in-tray exercise. When combined with interviews and other selection methods it becomes an assessment centre.

TRIAL RUN

Demonstrating skills within the somewhat artificial context of an assessment centre is one thing – demonstrating them on the job is another. An increasing number of organizations are finding opportunities for candidates to be assessed on real tasks within the organization before a firm appointment is made.

Prêt à Manger is a London-based fast food chain, founded in 1986 by two chartered surveyors who were dissatisfied with what most sandwich bars were offering. Now with 50 shops and a turnover of more than £70 million, the company prides itself on offering both service and food way above the standard of its competitors. How does it recruit staff? After an initial interview, which focuses on friendliness and team orientation, potential recruits are thrown in at the deep end – they work as a paid employee in a shop for a day. At the end of this trial period, the manager and staff decide whether or not the person will be offered a permanent post. Peter Armitage, human resources director, says:

> Our criteria are simple: they must be a Prêt person. They must have the right personality to work for us, which applies whether recruits are coming in to a senior IT role or as a team member in a shop.

Giving potential employees a trial run is equally applicable to senior staff. When UK pharmaceutical company Hydron was looking for a new senior manager, it thought it had found the ideal candidate. But as a final check, he was asked to spend two days at work in the company. By the end of the two days, he had alienated everyone from shopfloor workers to senior colleagues with his pushy and abrasive style of working. With sighs of relief, the company invited the number two candidate to go through the same process and he passed with flying colours. Companies which use this approach inevitably discover that they find out far more about the person by seeing them doing the real job than they do in the somewhat artificial setting of an interview or assessment centre.

The danger of practical tests and trial runs is that they can be used in an undisciplined way. Each part of the selection process is useful only if it provides you with information to answer the question: 'Does this candidate have the technical skills, the people skills and the values we are looking for?' You should do nothing in the selection process unless it gives you high quality information in these areas.

Choosing between candidates who come along to meet you is all very well, but you have to meet them first. High trust organizations want to attract the best in their field, and so they make sure they trawl widely for potential new recruits. New technology offers some interesting opportunities for this.

MAKE IT EASY FOR THE RIGHT PEOPLE TO APPLY

When *Computerworld* magazine polled information systems managers from over 1000 US companies to determine the best place to work for computer people, Cisco took the top spot. The company, a global supplier of computer software, has grown from 250 employees in 1990 to over 7000 now – and it is still growing. How has it managed to recruit the right staff to fuel such phenomenal growth? It has a Web page which carries information about job opportunities, company culture and values, and remuneration and benefits. There is a facility for people to apply electronically, either by e-mailing their CV or by completing an on-line application form.

But Cisco goes further than this. It also advertises in newspapers, partly to give the address of its Web site, but also to promote its 'friends' network. If you already know someone at Cisco, you can send them your resumé and network with them. But if you don't know anyone at Cisco, go to the Web page, fill in an on-line form, and Cisco will connect you with a 'friend' who does the same kind of work as you. Each day, Cisco's HR department matches these enquiries with volunteers from within the company. The volunteer phones the person up, chats, answers questions and e-mails the company recruiters that the person has been 'befriended'. If the candidate is subsequently hired, the volunteer gets a referral bonus.

Using the Internet is particularly appropriate for Cisco because of the kind of people it wants to recruit. Recruiting on the Internet may not be appropriate for your company – at least not yet. But the principle remains: make it easy for the kind of people you want to attract to apply for jobs with your organization.

MAKE IT A TWO-WAY PROCESS

The recruitment process must be two way. It should give the candidates the information they need to decide whether they want to work for your company, as well as giving the company the information it needs to choose the best candidate.

Each year Texas Instruments (TI) recruits about 200 college graduates. It used to do this by inviting final-year students to sit a three-hour assessment which rigorously tested all the technical skills which TI wanted from its graduate intake. Unfortunately, not only did the students hate doing it, but it wasn't a very reliable way of identifying 200 superb students. TI scrapped the test and instead offers students a computer disk called 'Engineer Your Career'. The program gives information about TI and invites students to answer 32 questions about their preferences for working conditions, teamwork and so on. The disk then tells the student how closely their preferences match what TI has on offer. Following this section there is a built-in CV writer which helps the student to complete a CV, and an up-to-date list of current vacancies with the company. All students who complete the program and mail it back receive feedback, whether or not they are asked to attend an interview as the next step towards joining the company. Dan McMurtey at TI's human resources department comments:

> Even if the individual doesn't want to come and work with us, we've given them a useful self help kit. After completing the program, many do decide to self select out, and that's good. It's going to increase the quality of the face to face interviews we do.

PUTTING IN THE EFFORT

What's your reaction to the different approaches which high trust organizations use to recruit people? Is it excitement: here are some things you can adapt for your organization? Or is it a feeling that all this takes too much time and effort? High trust organizations *do* put a lot of time and effort into choosing people. When German automaker Mercedes-Benz was looking for 650 people to work in a new plant in Tuscaloosa, Alabama, it put thousands of potential candidates through over 80 hours of assessment. Hewlett-Packard puts potential new hires through at least seven interviews before making a job offer. And when British retailer Marks & Spencer decided to appoint a new finance director from outside the company, it put the eventually successful candidate Keith Oates through no less than 35 interviews.

The question is whether all this time and effort is justified. For high trust organizations it is. Spending 80 hours choosing a new recruit is a tiny amount of time compared to all that taken supervising and monitoring someone you can't trust. Seven – even 35 – interviews are a very modest investment compared to the damage that could be caused by putting someone in a top job who is not competent, open, reliable and equitable. Building relationships of trust takes time up front, but saves it later on.

LISTEN PERCEPTIVELY

How is it that some people seem to have an unerring instinct for assessing people accurately, while others constantly make errors of judgement? In this section we'll look at the skills you need to improve your powers of perception and judgement. Like any new skill, they might seem a little strange at first – but as you practise them more and more, they will become so habitual that you too will develop a reputation for having an 'instinct' for choosing the right people.

RAPPORT

What is **rapport**? When one person is prowling around angrily, shouting at another person who is cowering in a chair, then it's unlikely that they are in rapport. Equally, someone who is energetically trying to share their enthusiasm with another person who is more laid back and thoughtful isn't likely to have much rapport either. On the other hand, think about a couple who are enjoying a romantic evening in a restaurant – they probably are in rapport. What do you notice? They may use the same tone of voice, they may be in similar postures, they may be mirroring each other's gestures. In fact, when two people are deeply in rapport it's almost as if they are doing a sort of slow motion dance together.

When people are in rapport, they find it easier to build a relationship of trust. Being able to build rapport with someone is useful in just about any situation where you want to communicate with another person. It's particularly useful in a selection interview when it's important to both of you that some open and honest communication takes place.

One way to begin to build rapport with another person is simply to notice how quickly they talk. Do they talk in a very slow and considered way, with lots of pauses? If so, slow down your rate of speech until it matches theirs. Do they talk rapidly and energetically? In this case, speed up your speech rate until it is closer to theirs. Obviously this needs to be done in a respectful way – if you are merely mimicking the other person this is going to be highly irritating. But if you subtly match your rate of speech, and indeed body posture, to theirs, not only will the other person be more likely to trust you, but you are going to find it easier to 'step into the other person's shoes', to see the world the way they see it. Such perceptiveness is very useful indeed during any interview.

For some people, this is a new way of thinking about selection interviews. Build rapport? Be open and honest? Some interviewers think that the whole experience should be as stressful as possible. They take the view that by increasing the stress levels, they will be able to trip the candidates up and trick them into revealing their 'true selves'. This approach is based on a number of unhelpful beliefs, one of which is that people are more likely to be themselves under conditions of intense stress. Do you give the best of yourself when under extreme stress? Probably not – most people find that a certain amount of adrenalin can help performance, but if the stress is too great they tend to act in ways they later regret. People are not like tea bags – you don't have to put them into hot water to find out how good they are.

Stressful interviews

Creating stress in this way also gives the candidate the message that in this company relationships are based not on trust, but on power. We'll make it stressful for you, so that we can force you to say things you might not want to. If your company is based on power relationships, maybe it's no bad thing to give people a taste of that right from the word go. But if you are choosing people to join an organization which believes in the trust effect, then you have to be consistent with this in the way you recruit people.

Of course, I'm not suggesting that job interviews should be as relaxed as possible and take place on scatter cushions. A certain amount of formality is useful: but you will learn more about candidates if you make it a reasonably comfortable experience for everyone involved. Make sure that you introduce yourself, that candidates receive a genuine welcome, and that the physical surroundings are appropriate. All these have a part to play, but if you want to begin a relationship of trust, rapport is essential.

PUSH FOR SPECIFICS

Once you've got rapport, you can begin to ask questions. What type of questions will give you the kind of information you want? That depends on the kind of information you need. Naturally, you will structure your interview questions around the list of technical skills, people skills and values you are trying to find out about. But there is more to it than that. Consider these two statements:

> I had full responsibility for the marketing function's human resources.

> When I became marketing manager I found myself in charge of a team of three marketing officers. Two were very experienced and doing a good job; one was new and struggling.

Which tells your more about the person? The second statement not only tells you more, but it is a good deal more interesting to listen to. The first statement is too abstract, while the second is more like the beginning of a story.

Telling stories

In an interview, you want to get people telling you their stories. To get them to tell stories, ask them questions like:

- Give me an example of…

- Tell me about a time when…

- Please illustrate that point with an anecdote.

Of course, you don't just want stories, you want stories which are rich in **specific** information. Be alert to the possibilities of follow-up questions which ask for specifics. In the example above, useful follow-up questions would be:

- How experienced were the two marketing officers?

- How did you know they were doing a good job?

- In what way was the third person struggling?

- What did you do to help?

Skilful interviewers push candidates for specific examples;
poor ones are satisfied with vague statements like 'I took
an empowering approach' even though they don't really
have a notion of what the candidate means by such a
phrase.

Pushing for specifics gives you a great deal of information
about skills. To get at values, you need to go in the
opposite direction – ask people to draw some general
conclusions from the specific examples they have given
you. Once you have had the stories – and not before – ask
questions like:

DRAW CONCLUSIONS

- What does that say about you as a person?

- What general principles were you working to in that
  instance?

- What values do you think underpinned your actions in
  that case?

Give the person time to think. Remember that people are
often not consciously aware of the values and beliefs which
drive their behaviour and may need a moment or two to
decide on them. But given the opportunity – and the
rapport – people usually will say something illuminating.
And don't be worried that the person may have chosen
untypical examples of their behaviour. In nearly every case
they will talk about what they usually do – our brains work
like that.

LOOK FOR CONSISTENCY

Rapport, pushing for specifics and drawing out conclusions will give you masses of useful information. There's one final thing you can do which will really put the icing on the interview cake. Look for **consistency**. When we talk, we communicate through our words, the tone of our voice and the way we move our body – what is often called 'body language'. If all three 'channels' are giving a consistent message, you can be fairly sure that the information is reliable. But if there's a mismatch, then you need to probe further. Incidentally, that's how lie detectors work – most people sweat more when they are being deceitful and a lie detector simply measures this change in skin moisture. You don't need a gadget like this because when people are being economical with the truth it often shows itself in more blatant ways.

I once watched a TV programme about the British toy company which had turned down the rights to market the Teenage Mutant Ninja Turtles. The man responsible for this decision was interviewed and he described how this error of judgement had lost the company millions, and that furthermore they'd thrown good money after bad by trying to promote a rival product called Bucky O'Hare, which had not been nearly as successful. Despite all of this, the man said that he wasn't bothered by his mistake and that the company could do without the turtles. Throughout the interview he maintained a broad smile – a grin, in fact. The inconsistency between his tale of woe and the smile was painful. The inappropriateness and insincerity of the smile spoke volumes to me – I suspect that he was very upset indeed by the whole episode. His interview didn't do much to inspire trust. On the other hand, when the cameras turned to the man who'd developed the turtles idea he came across as totally consistent. He smiled when he was describing the fun he'd had developing them, and looked serious when describing setbacks in the project.

So what do you do if you spot inconsistency during an interview? Ask for more information. You might even ask about the inconsistency itself. This can be very revealing.

CULTURE AND CHOICE

Your choice of what you are looking for in a potential new employee – and the way you go about finding him or her – is highly influenced by your national culture. In some national cultures, the USA and the Netherlands for example, it is generally accepted that the best way to begin a new business relationship is to get straight to the point as soon as possible. The first question in a job interview might be a polite enquiry about the journey there, but after that it's straight in to a discussion of whether the candidate has the skills and qualities which the potential employer wants.

Other cultures take a different approach. In Japan, Mexico, France and much of southern Europe, it is generally believed that it is much better to get to know the person, before getting down to the specifics of the particular job. Job interviews are much more likely to talk at length about a person's life outside work as well as in it.

Neither approach is demonstrably superior to the other, but it is as well to be aware of the difference. When a US company is trying to establish a business partnership with a Japanese firm, the Americans may experience the Japanese as evasive – they seem to want to engage in endless pleasantries and chitchat instead of getting down to firming up the deal. On the other hand, the Japanese may experience the Americans as blunt and naïve – how can you enter into a business relationship of trust unless you have taken the time to get to know your partners first?

CHOOSING SUPPLIERS

Choosing the right employees is important in a high trust organization, and so is choosing the right supplier. If you make the wrong choice you may be saddled with poor quality, unreliable delivery times and the possibility of interruptions to supplies. If the supplier is providing you with an intangible service – an advertising campaign, advice on a new computer system, management consultancy – the consequences of a poor choice can easily spell the end of your organization.

The traditional method of choosing a supplier goes something like this: write out the specification for the thing you want supplied; put it out to tender; choose the lowest bid. Let's say your company needs a new brochure printed on an annual basis. Every year you put the job out to tender. You accept the lowest bid. You expect there to be problems with delivery times and quality, because there always are. And you convince yourself that the time it takes to go through that tendering process each year is justified, because it 'keeps the printers on their toes'.

This traditional way of choosing suppliers is about as effective as the traditional way of choosing employees, on the basis of one short, ill-planned interview. High trust organizations aim to develop long-term relationships with their suppliers which provide both quality and low costs. Because they aim for long-term relationships they don't have to choose suppliers very often, but when they do they are very thorough. They use the same three skills that we have already seen in the context of choosing employees – they clarify what they want, they listen perceptively, and they design a process to get what they want.

When Toyota was ready to introduce the luxury Lexus brand into the USA it already had one of the strongest dealer networks in the country. But the company knew that it wanted something more than this – its aim was to establish a level of relationship marketing the US auto industry had never seen. In order to do this it decided to set up an entirely new dealer network for the Lexus. The process for finding this involved identifying an initial pool of some 1500 possible dealers. A perceptive screening process eventually resulted in 150 dealers being appointed.

SAYING GOODBYE

High trust organizations are not cavalier when it comes to firing people; in fact, they try to avoid it whenever they can. Hewlett-Packard's Dave Packard often recalled with pride the time he turned down a highly lucrative contract because it would have involved heavy hiring at the outset and heavy firing after the job was completed. But high trust organizations *are* very tough when they have to deal with people who cannot live up to expectations. Management writer Charles Handy comments:

Tough trust

> Even the best recruiters and the best judges of character will get it wrong sometimes. When trust proves to be misplaced – not because people are deceitful or malicious but because they do not live up to expectations or cannot be relied upon to do what is needed – then those people have to go. Where you cannot trust, you have to become a checker once more, with all the systems of control that involves. Therefore, for the sake of the whole, the individual must leave. Trust has to be ruthless.

In essence, high trust organizations expect staff to do two things – to get results and to adhere to a set of values. They hold people accountable. That means that if people are consistently failing in either of these areas, then it's time for the organization to ask them to leave. Because high trust organizations rely so much on the quality and consistency of their people, only strong performers who retain the company's confidence will continue to have a career within that organization.

Semco is a Brazilian engineering firm with an international reputation for the extraordinary degree to which it is run on trust, as we will see in the case below. There is no organizational chart, little in the way of rules, all financial information is openly shared, and some staff even set their own salaries. Every six months, managers are evaluated by the people they supervise, who anonymously complete a multi-choice questionnaire. The grades are posted for all to see. While there are no hard and fast rules, those who consistently receive poor marks (80% is average) sooner or later leave the company.

High trust organizations want not just high performers, they want people who are willing to live the organization's values. First Direct's former chief executive Kevin Newman explains:

> Successful organizations are those which are able to institutionalize their values. They don't depend on a charismatic leader – everyone in the business lives by the values. When someone acts counter to those values it's like an infection in the bloodstream – everyone else acts like white blood cells to cluster around and help the person to change – or to leave.

There's an intensity about working in a high trust organization which some people find exhilarating. Others, however, are not able to cope – and they have to go.

CHOOSING PEOPLE AT SEMCO

Promotion to management roles at Semco is decided not by more senior managers, but by potential subordinates. President Ricardo Semler describes how Anatoly Timoshenko won his promotion.

'As Timoshenko entered the room, the chatter from the several dozen people who had assembled there ceased. Timoshenko opened the meeting by calmly pointing out that antagonism had been built into his last job. Yes, he had pushed too hard. Yes, he had made mistakes. But he would change.

There were a few nods, but most of the people just sat there in stony silence. After a while, Almir asked to speak. His talents as an electrical engineer were well known. So were his candour and temper. True to his reputation, he angrily accused Timoshenko of mishandling the assignment and placing his own ambition first.

A few factory supervisors tried to defend Timoshenko, but the engineers and the administrative people kept up their attack. As the afternoon wore on, it became clear that Almir and some of the other engineers might quit if Timoshenko were promoted. A few resignations and the core of the technological backbone would be lost. Orders for biscuit machinery were already stacking up. If the engineers prevailed, we would lose Timoshenko. If Timoshenko won, we might lose some engineers. Despite the value of these technocrats, we decided we would abide by the outcome. Democracy would prevail, and we trusted, Semco would too.

Judgement day arrived, and the three factions took their accustomed places in the room. After an hour of discussion, each employee took a questionnaire and began filling it in. Soon enough, the results were read aloud, group by group. First came the engineers. Interestingly, their low grades on the questions involving interpersonal relations were partially offset by better marks on questions concerning Timoshenko's technical competence. Next came the factory workers. All their grades were exceptionally high, prompting muttering from the engineers. The marks from the administrative people were in between.

When the results were calculated Timoshenko had a 74 – four more points than he needed. In the end no one resigned. And Timoshenko eventually made a surprising selection for the job of chief engineer, the person who would be his right arm – the utterly flabbergasted Almir. Soon he and Timoshenko were working on a budget for a unit that would become one of our great successes.'

Source: Semler, Ricardo (1993) *Maverick*, Century.

Tell Them the Score 4

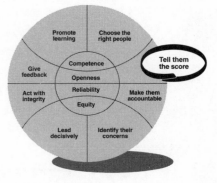

In my experience, relationships and loyalty have
become undervalued commodities at many American
companies. So many of us have lost sight of the vital
importance of dealing with people we can trust.
Adversarial or distant relationships are not inevitable –
nor are they the best way of doing business. There is
much to be gained by enlisting partners and colleagues
who are committed to the same goals.

Howard Schultz, Chairman and CEO, Starbucks

*O*NCE you have the right people for your organization,
you need to make sure that you are open with them.
Why do high trust organizations value openness? There are
two reasons. First, you can't have relationships based on
trust, with all the advantages which the trust effect brings,
unless you are open with people. Secrecy and
deviousness are anathema to trust. Secondly, you can't
expect people to be able to contribute in any meaningful
way to an organization unless they know what they are
contributing to. As management writer Douglas McGregor
wrote:

Effective performance results when the conditions are created such that the members of the organization can achieve their own goals best by directing their efforts towards the success of the enterprise.

If people are going to direct their efforts towards the success of the enterprise, they need to know how the enterprise judges success, hence the need to tell them the score. Many companies think they are doing this simply by posting a mission statement prominently on the office wall. But mission statements are generally little more than expressions of intent – and they are regarded not infrequently with deep cynicism by the workers. Telling people the score means much more than this. It means communicating to everyone in the organization its key values and the objectives against which progress is measured. Before you can communicate them, you need to know what they are.

UNDERSTAND VALUES

When you ask about your organization's values, you get to the heart of what the organization is about. For some organizations, the answer is quite simple. When financier James Goldsmith was attempting to take over the Akron, Ohio-based tyre firm Goodyear, he was accused of being in business solely to make profit. He replied:

> I can think of no finer reason for doing business ... I strongly recommend that the United States, which was built on that idea, remain on that idea.

An alternative view of what businesses exist to do was put forward by Hewlett-Packard co-founder Dave Packard. In 1960 he said to a group of staff:

> I want to discuss why a company exists in the first place. I think many people assume, wrongly, that a company exists solely to make money. While this is an

important result of a company's existence, we have to go deeper and find the real reasons for our being. As we investigate this, we inevitably come to the conclusion that a group of people gets together and exists as an institution we call a company so they are able to accomplish something collectively that they could not accomplish separately – they make a contribution to society, a phrase which sounds trite but is fundamental.

For Hewlett-Packard, being able to make a technical contribution to society is a fundamental value which guides everything they do. So much so that H-P has turned down business which might have made it plenty of money, but offered no scope for making a technical contribution.

High trust organizations exist not just to make money, but to fulfil a set of values. Consider the story of AES. Roger Sant and Dennis Bakke originally formed Applied Energy Services as a consultancy to provide advice on setting up clean, safe and reliable power stations. However, they thought it might be interesting to found a corporation to practise what they were preaching, and so AES was born. The company now operates five power plants. AES has four key values which are integral to everything it does – fun, fairness, integrity and social responsibility.

Social responsibility is a tricky issue to put into practice in a power generation company. AES uses mainly coal-fired power stations and, despite using the most up-to-date 'clean coal' technology available, there is inherent damage to the environment. So in the late 1980s chairman Roger Sant set up a task force to see what could be done. In cooperation with local development agencies, AES funded a project to plant 54 million trees in Guatemala, sufficient to offset all the carbon dioxide emissions from the entire 40-year life of an AES plant. The tree planting project cost more than a year's operating profit for the company. The company's prospectus states:

Earning a fair profit is an important result of providing a quality product to customers. However, when a perceived conflict has arisen between these values and profits, the company has tried to adhere to its values – even though so doing might result in diminished profits or foregone opportunities. The company seeks to adhere to these values, not as a means to achieve economic success, but because adherence is a worthwhile goal in itself.

Although the values of a high trust organization will vary in their specific detail, in essence they are all rooted in the CORE principles of the trust effect – competence, openness, reliability and equity.

All high trust organizations identify their chosen field of competence. For H-P it is technical excellence in the electronics field; for Johnson & Johnson it is to alleviate pain and distress. All high trust organizations have a commitment to openness – often expressed in terms of honesty or integrity. All high trust organizations have a commitment to reliability, often expressed in terms of customer satisfaction. All high trust organizations have a commitment to equity, often expressed in terms of meeting the needs of the different stakeholders.

Stakeholders

Stakeholders are the people affected by the actions of your organization. They generally include customers, suppliers, financial backers, employees and members of the local community. The effect of the company on the natural environment is often also part of the equation. The stakeholder idea came to prominence in the UK with a report by the London-based Royal Society for the encouragement of Arts, Manufactures and Commerce (RSA). The RSA brought together 25 of the UK's top businesses under the leadership of Sir Anthony Cleaver, then Chairman of IBM UK. The objective was to develop a shared vision of tomorrow's company. In a report published under that name, the RSA came down firmly in favour of a stakeholder perspective:

The conventional wisdom in the UK is to define the purpose of business in terms which stress the importance of immediate financial performance and returns to shareholders. Of course a board must continually attend to its company's financial performance and level of shareholder return, but an exclusive concentration on any one stakeholder will not lead to sustainable competitive performance. We believe that sustainable success is available from the inclusive approach in which the company includes all its relationships in its definitions and measures of success. A winning company must inspire its people to new levels of skill, efficiency and creativity, supported by a sense of shared destiny with customers, suppliers and investors.

This perspective was given a further boost by British prime minister Tony Blair while still in opposition, when he said:

We cannot by legislation guarantee that a company will behave in a way conducive to trust and long term commitment. But is it surely time to assess how we shift the emphasis in corporate ethos from the company being a mere vehicle for the capital market to be traded, bought and sold as a commodity, towards a vision of the company as a community or partnership in which each employee has a stake, and where the company's responsibilities are more clearly delineated.

Stakeholding as a concept is nothing new in the US. Johnson & Johnson's credo, its statement of business values, acknowledges the company's responsibility to its customers, employees, managers, communities and stockholders – in that order. This was drafted by RW Johnson in 1943. And a commitment to equity as a core value is both nice to have and profitable. When Harvard Business School researchers John Kotter and James Heskett surveyed 200 large US companies, they found that the ones which did best financially were those which paid most attention to the needs of all their stakeholders. The 12 firms in the survey which paid attention to all stakeholders increased their net profits by an average of 70 per cent annually over the 11-year period of the survey.

UNDERSTAND OBJECTIVES

Understanding objectives is easy – at least for the people at the top of the organization. Since every organization needs cash to survive, financial objectives should always be part of the equation. However, financial objectives are what is known in the trade as a lagging indicator. They are very good at telling you where the business has been, but are less useful in determining where it is going. It's like navigating a ship just by looking behind at the wake.

Balanced scorecard

Robert Kaplan and David Norton originated the notion of a 'balanced scorecard'. They claim that companies should set themselves objectives not only in terms of finance, but in terms of customer satisfaction, quality and innovation. In this way, they argue, those leading the company will have a more rounded and reliable view of what is happening. Many private sector companies do operate according to such objectives, although they may not use the same terminology.

Public sector

The position for public sector bodies is sometimes more difficult. Traditionally, many public sector bodies – local government, schools, hospitals, charities – have been extremely reluctant to set measurable objectives. If you don't have measurable objectives you can't communicate them to your employees, customers and financial backers – you can't tell them the score. The price you pay for this is a lack of trust; indeed, trust often seems even more elusive in the public sector than it is in the private sector. Many people who work in not-for-profit organizations believe that you can't measure the success of whatever they are doing – that education, healthcare or the relief of poverty are somehow not susceptible to being measured. This view is not shared by the people who fund such bodies, who, not unreasonably, impose their own measures of success on the organizations they fund. But having to work to someone else's success measures – when you yourself don't believe in the concept – is hardly a recipe for trust. Setting measures of success at the organizational and team level is no harder in the public and voluntary sector than it is in the private sector. Both sectors work to financial measures, which are generally easy to define, and to other objectives which require a little more thought to measure correctly.

The way out of this dilemma is for public and voluntary agencies to be much more proactive in setting their own success measures. This is exactly what has happened in Indianapolis. The municipal government has made measurable progress in the last five years: operating budget down 7 per cent, taxes cut twice, $700 million invested in roads, sewers and infrastructure and an increase in the public safety budget of more than 40 per cent. One of the ways the city has achieved this is by telling staff the score, particularly in relation to financial matters. For example, when the Public Works Department analysed its costs, it discovered that the city had spent $252,000 on repairs to a garbage truck which cost $90,000 when new. The city garage which maintained the truck had had no reason to track costs.

When the city started setting team performance measures, it discovered that huge advances were possible. Most urban areas have a problem with abandoned cars, usually in poor neighbourhoods. They are unsightly and dangerous. In 1993, the city towed away 900 vehicles, representing about one-tenth of the complaints received. The service cost the city's taxpayers $174,000 a year. When the service was contracted out to a car auction company, 2300 vehicles were removed, generating a net income for the city of over $500,000, while dramatically improving the service to neighbourhood residents.

Proactivity

SHARE THE KNOWLEDGE

Simply understanding your organization's values and objectives is not enough – you have to share them with every employee. Telling people the score enhances trust because you are being more open. It also enhances trust because it enables people to be more competent.

When organizations withhold business information from staff, they prevent them from taking effective decisions. This puts staff in the predicament of either having to guess or to take the decision up the management hierarchy, with all the time delays and added costs which that implies. Worse than that, the very act of withholding information creates a climate of uncertainty and mistrust. Anyone who has worked in a company where there are rumours of big redundancies or other major organizational change, and the top managers refuse to give any information, will know just how destructive of trust this is.

Mushroom management

And yet, withholding business information from staff is so common that it has even spawned its own jargon – mushroom management. A polite definition of this is to keep staff in the dark and occasionally throw manure at them. In the days when the world of work was far less competitive, organizations could afford to restrict information to a few senior managers, who filtered it down to front-line staff. These days, things are different – customers expect an instant and knowledgeable response from the person they are dealing with and don't want to be fobbed off while the enquiry is passed to some inaccessible manager. As well as losing customers, it simply costs too much to filter information through layers of hierarchy – it is cheaper, and more effective, to make it available directly to front-line staff.

COMMUNICATING VALUES

How is knowledge shared in high trust organizations? First, how do you communicate your organization's values to staff? By publishing them in the staff handbook? Engraving them on tablets of stone? These actions in themselves are not enough. You have to demonstrate these values consistently in everything you do. In some ways this is quite difficult. The company's policies, its public image, the way it deals with customers, suppliers, members of the local community, the way it recruits people, the kind of training programmes it offers, the way managers relate to staff, the company structures and systems, the actions of everyone associated with the company every minute of the day all need to be consistent with the organization's values.

Achieving this level of consistency is quite tough. But in another way, living by a set of values can make some decisions very easy. As we'll see later in the book, Johnson & Johnson boss Jim Burke lost no sleep over a decision which deprived the company of an annual income of $100 million, because the alternative did not accord with J&J's values.

In contrast to telling the score in relation to values, telling the score in relation to objectives is easier. High trust organizations make sure that all staff are given information about how success is measured. In small companies this is easy to do. Airedale Springs Ltd is a Yorkshire-based manufacturer which employs 100 staff making components for the automotive industry. Wall displays which chart the company's success are updated every week. Every employee can see how the company is doing in terms of production and delivery targets.

Larger organizations need to be more systematic. Marks & Spencer ensures that its annual results appear in the staff newsletter just as soon as they are released, and further information is provided on a store-by-store basis.

But this kind of information is meaningless unless everyone can understand it, so education is important as well as information giving. In most businesses there are two kinds of people: those who speak the language of finance and those who don't. Those who do are usually a small minority of senior managers and finance specialists. To them, running any enterprise without 'the numbers' is incomprehensible. They realize that unless close attention

COMMUNICATING OBJECTIVES

is given to profit margins, cash flow and working capital the business will never survive; they also know that the financials are the ultimate measure of failure or success. The majority of people in the company do not understand finance, however. They may have a vague understanding that the business has to make a profit to continue in existence, but they are probably unaware that many businesses go to the wall because they run out of cash, even though they are profitable. If they looked at the company's balance sheet they would either find it completely incomprehensible or, worse still, misleading. As a result, the level of trust falls. The financial literates can't understand why everyone else complains about cost cutting or financial discipline; the financial illiterates can't understand why money is so tight when there seem to be plenty of customers and top managers earning big salaries and driving fancy cars. As trust drops, so does motivation.

Increasingly organizations are realizing the value of teaching all staff the basics of financial literacy. This ensures that everyone is able to understand the financial measures the company uses to gauge success.

Managers are sometimes reluctant to share information about financial performance if the news is bad. Surely this will simply drive morale lower, they argue. If the company is performing poorly, staff will pick that up through the grapevine – managers who put a brave face on it and pretend that everything is fine will simply lose more credibility and trust. In these situations, it is even more important to share knowledge openly with staff.

In 1991 Britain, in common with many other countries, was in the depths of a recession – one which drove many companies out of business altogether. Airedale Springs was faced with a difficult decision: should it make redundancies or impose a pay cut? One or other was vital to cut costs in the short term; both could be damaging in the long term. Chairman Michael Parkinson gathered the workforce together in the canteen and explained the dilemma he was facing. He asked the workforce for their views. Clearly they weren't happy, but because of the high levels of trust which existed in the company – in part because of the open sharing of information – the staff chose to take a pay cut. The company pulled through with its skilled workforce intact, and was able to reinstate salary levels six months later.

If baseball fans or cricket enthusiasts were unable to understand the scoring system, and had no idea which side was winning or losing, what would that do to their interest in the game? It would plummet! Of course people watch sport because of the satisfaction of watching players demonstrate outstanding skills, but ultimately it's the score which adds excitement and makes the sport worth watching. The same is true of business – if people don't understand whether their company is winning or losing, then a lot of the excitement, energy and motivation disappears.

SPRINGFIELD REMANUFACTURING

One company which has been outstandingly successful at telling the score is Springfield Remanufacturing Corporation. When Jack Stack took over at Springfield Remanufacturing Corporation (SRC) in 1984 he inherited 119 disgruntled employees, a company which was losing $60,000 a year and a mountain of debt. Ten years later SRC employed 650 staff and had annual profits of $1.8 million.

Put yourself in the shoes of an employee at an engineering plant. In front of you sits a messy, broken piece of equipment – part of a diesel engine perhaps. You ask yourself should you fix it or scrap it? In most companies, such a decision would be right out of the hands of hourly paid employees. This decision would be down to the supervisor or the production manager. In some companies this is even a policy matter, decided by senior management. At SRC the employee decides because he or she knows the exact financial

consequences of rework versus scrap for this item –
the financial consequences for the company and for
the individual's pay packet. Let's take a close look at
how SRC has got to this position, and see what
lessons are transferable to your situation.

After Stack had begun the task of building trust
with his colleagues at SRC by inviting them to paint
their work areas in whatever way they wanted, he
made a start on teaching financial literacy. One day,
he shut the plant and called everyone to the
Springfield Hilton Inn for what was billed as an
Employee Awareness Day. This is what he told them:

'Most people have the wrong idea about business as
being terribly dull and serious – really it is just a game,
no more complicated than baseball or golf. The
difference is, the stakes are higher. How you play golf
determines whether you get a trophy or not; how you
play "the Great Game of Business" determines whether
you can pay the mortgage, put food on the table and
fulfil your dreams. To be frank I don't think wealth is
distributed fairly in this country or around the world. To
me, it's inexcusable for Lee Iacocca to pay himself
$4.5 million a year at the same time he's laying off
thousands of employees, and he is by no means the
worst offender. On the other hand, I don't think we can
solve the problems by taking away Iacocca's millions.
That's really just a drop in the bucket. The only way to
solve these problems long term is to make people
conscious of generating profits and understanding
profits, where profits come from and where they go.
Somebody's got to be out there teaching people about
wealth – about retained earnings, about equity, about
an earnings multiple and what it means and how it can
affect them individually. If we don't do it, we will never
increase our standard of living. We'll remain in this
ignorant, dormant stage where we continually think a
job is a job is a job. And the decline will continue.'

For the rest of the day, people divided into small groups and attended workshops run by the different departments. The idea was that every member of staff would get the 'big picture' about how the business fitted together and how each individual contributed.

After this introductory day, SRC's staff were ready to learn all about the Great Game of Business. An intensive period of education and training followed. All staff attended formal training sessions on business finance. Managers began coaching their own staff about how each individual affected the overall profitability of SRC. At the same time, there was a programme of internal visits and job swaps so that staff could continue to develop their understanding of the big picture. Already staff motivation and profitability were shooting upwards at SRC. Stack recalls one typical example, the warehouse supervisor who, as it happens, was called Bill Clinton:

'For a long time Billy thought he was an insignificant nobody, a cog in the wheel. He thought his job was to hold onto parts until somebody else needed them. But when he educated himself in the language of numbers, he began to understand his role. He saw instantly how much money was lost when an assembly line went down. A couple of times, the line went down because nobody could find some parts that were supposedly in the warehouse. It dawned on Billy that the organization was depending on him to know exactly what was available. If his counts were inaccurate, we might run low on a critical part without knowing it. In effect, he and his people were keeping the assembly lines up and running by having accurate inventory counts. The plant really needed them to grow. I can't tell you what a revelation that is to somebody. Suddenly what he does has meaning. It's not work; it's not a job; it's a responsibility. And it's food on his family's table.'

Despite the dramatic improvement at SRC, Stack was not prepared to stop there; he had yet to put into practice his fundamental belief that the best, most efficient, most profitable way to operate a business is to give everybody in the company a voice in saying how the company is run.

The next step was to establish the huddle system. Every Wednesday morning, about 50 managers, supervisors and other people from the company meet in the conference room of SRC's office building. Each person in attendance announces their numbers from the previous week, and everyone notes them down on a scorecard. When all the scores are in, the chief financial officer announces the overall tally – the profit. The Great Huddle, as it is known, means that 50 people instantly know how well the company is doing and why. They go back to their own departments and immediately brief their staff on what is happening. Within a matter of hours, everyone knows how SRC is doing, and who has contributed what to that.

Over the next few days, each team will discuss what it can do to improve the numbers. How do they do this? By relating their own set of performance goals to the financial measures of the company as a whole. The results of these discussions – part formal meetings, part informal chatter – are finalized by Tuesday afternoon. Each department is then ready to send its representative to the next Great Huddle on Wednesday morning with a revised set of figures.

What are the benefits of the huddle system? First, it gives people very quick feedback about how the business is doing. If the company looks at the financials only once a month, or even once a quarter, that's going to be quite an inaccurate way of directing the business. Secondly, it puts the decision making where it should be – with the people who will have to carry out those decisions.

The final element of open book management as practised at SRC is the bonus system – universally referred to at the company at STP-GUTR, pronounced stop-gooter. Its name derived from a comment which an SRC employee made to Stack in the early days of playing the Great Game: Skip The Praise – Give Us The Raise. All SRC employees are remunerated in three ways: a base salary which is a fair reward for doing a decent job, a bonus system which can be worth up to 18 per cent of base pay, and an employee share ownership scheme which gives staff a stake in the equity of the company. The maths of the bonus system at SRC are a little complicated, but the principles are these. Each year the company sets two or three financial targets – they might be profit, liquidity and debt. For each goal, different levels of bonus payouts are set for different levels of achievement of that goal. Each quarter, results are measured and if the company has hit the goals, staff receive a bonus payment. Any unearned bonus payments are rolled over into the next quarter, so that if the company fails to hit any targets for the first three months, but catches up in the next three so that it is on course by the end of six months, then the staff can still earn all of their bonus payments. The same thinking applies to each quarter of the year – in theory the company could underperform for the first nine months of the year but meet all annual targets with a spectacular last quarter, in which case staff would receive all their bonus payments.

Source: Stack, Jack (1992) *The Great Game of Business*, Currency Doubleday.

SRC has gained a lot from this approach. Annual profits are now of the order of $2 million and SRC stock worth 10 cents at the time of the buyout is now worth over $20 – an increase of 20,000 per cent, making many SRC employees very wealthy individuals. How much of this is applicable to your organization?

Education

The first step in telling people the score is to educate all staff about the measures of business success. In SRC's case, this means teaching people finances. You can do the same. How much financial detail you need to teach depends on the organization. In an enterprise like SRC which is all about wealth generation, people need the in-depth knowledge which enables them to take everyday decisions in the confidence that they are contributing to more wealth creation. On the other hand, in the public sector, staff need only a basic grasp of the finances. It is much more important to educate them on the non-financial measures which the organization uses to chart its achievement.

Feedback

The second step in telling people the score is to give staff rapid and regular feedback on how they are contributing to this success. At SRC, which is essentially located in one town, the huddle system works well for this. You need to give your team rapid and regular feedback on how they are achieving their team goals. The more you can relate this feedback to the overall success of the organization, the better – that's what team goals are for. Doing this might involve a short meeting once a week. It might involve posting information on your company's e-mail. It might involve regularly updated charts and diagrams displayed on the walls of your team's base. How you do it depends on your own circumstances – making it happen is what counts. Some people are a little jittery about giving employees too much information about the company as a whole, lest it fall into the wrong hands – those of competitors, for example. In practice, this rarely happens.

Share the rewards

The third step in telling people the score is sharing the rewards. Many high trust organizations do have some form of profit sharing, Nordstrom, Hewlett-Packard, Wal-Mart, Marks & Spencer, Northern Foods and Johnson & Johnson to name but a few. Sharing wealth with employees in such a direct way certainly doesn't harm trust, but it is not essential. For many public sector organizations – hospitals, colleges, arts organizations – profit sharing doesn't make much sense. What is crucial to trust is that employee remuneration must be seen to be fair. That's why, with a few exceptions – Nordstrom is one of them – high trust organizations usually don't go in much for individual performance-related pay. It's just too difficult to make fair judgements about individual performance and its link to pay.

WHAT IF YOU'RE NOT THE CEO?

In this chapter we've talked about the importance of telling people the score to create the kind of openness which is characteristic of a high trust organization. But what if you don't know the score yourself? What if the information about your company's financial and other objectives is a closed book to you?

Your first step is an obvious one – tell your team members what you *do* know. Better still, work with them to reach agreement on what the values and objectives of your team are. Make sure that you and your team members live by these values and measure your progress against these objectives. Then go to your boss and say, 'I've got a set of values and objectives here for my team, but I don't know whether achieving them is going to do the company any good, because, frankly, I don't know what values and objectives the company as a whole is working towards.'

Communicate what you do know

If your boss can help you, all well and good. If your boss can't, find someone else in the company who can. If no one in the company can help you, start looking for another job – because there's clearly an inconsistency between your values and the values of your organization.

Make Them Accountable 5

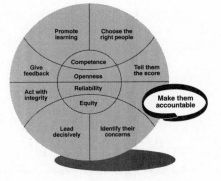

*R*ELIABILITY is part of the CORE of the trust effect. In fact for some people trust *is* reliability: you trust people because you can depend on them. Reliability is also a crucial ingredient of any successful business. Your customers are only going to keep coming back if you consistently provide them with what they want. The concept of total quality management was founded on this idea in the 1950s and is now well understood by most successful companies. A key tenet of total quality management is that if you want to deliver reliably to your external customers, then everyone inside the organization has to deliver reliably to each other, and your suppliers have to deliver reliably to you. So how can you achieve this desirable state of affairs?

Low trust organizations think they know how to make people reliable: they tell them exactly what to do every step of the way and they supervise and monitor them to ensure the job gets done. Workers might as well hang their brains up with their coats at the factory gate, only to collect them again when it's time to go home – they just have to do what they are told.

Frederick Taylor, the 'father' of scientific management, was fond of telling workers: 'You are not supposed to think. Other people are paid for thinking around here.' For Taylor, who developed his ideas on management at the turn of the twentieth century, the cardinal principle of running any effective enterprise was specialization. Each individual worker had his or her job to do, and it was set out in great detail. Workers were not expected to think or make decisions – that's what managers were paid for. Taylor's thinking has made a deep impression on the way many companies are organized, even today.

This approach produces results up to a point, but it is a very expensive way of doing business. High trust organizations know that there is another way to ensure that everyone acts reliably – and that is to make them **accountable** for their actions. This doesn't mean that managers should abdicate all their responsibilities and simply let their people get on with it (as some advocates of empowerment would recommend). Instead, managers must make sure that their people have all the resources they need to do the job, so that holding them accountable is a fair and sensible thing to do. In this chapter, we'll look at the skills you need to be able to do this. But first, let's take a look at some of your beliefs.

DO YOU BELIEVE IT IS POSSIBLE?

The rewards of trusting people at work are very great. High trust organizations get more commitment, better decision making and lower costs. Managers who make their staff truly accountable can expect less stress and better results. Just think how frustrating it would be if your boss were constantly checking your work, insisting that she was personally involved in everything that you do – and how liberating it would feel to know that she really trusted you.

Given all the advantages of giving more responsibility to staff, why is it that so many managers find it difficult to do this? Is it because they are power crazy? A tiny minority of managers may genuinely be power crazy, but most are not. The majority of managers do care about their staff, do want customers to have a good service and do want the company as a whole to be successful and profitable. What stops them trusting staff is their beliefs. Remember the manager at the financial services company in Chapter 2? He was able to make his staff accountable and build relationships based on trust, but his beliefs stopped him from doing it in the long term. Let's look at a few of the beliefs which might get in the way of trusting people.

I'm indispensable

If you start to trust people, you're going to spend less time checking, supervising and monitoring. This means that you probably won't be as busy as you were before. Now for some people, this is great – for others it is a rather daunting prospect, because of a deeply held belief that: 'If I'm busy I must be indispensable'. In an increasingly insecure workplace, many managers feel at some level that they have to take on a bigger workload in order to demonstrate their worth to the company. But is this a useful belief to hold? How many hours, exactly, do you have to work to guarantee job security? Do you know people who have lost their jobs even though they worked extremely hard? Isn't it true that these days, it is results that count, not how much effort you put into achieving them? On your deathbed, will you say: 'I wish I had spent more time at work' … or will you wish that you had spent more time with your family, having fun, learning a new sport or whatever?

There's no one I can trust

OK, I hear you say, I don't hold this belief at all – I work hard because I have to, there is no one I can delegate to, there is no one I can trust. This too is a belief. How useful a belief is it? What happens when you are on holiday, or ill? What would happen if, for some reason, you were absent from work for a few months? Would your department grind to a halt, or would some of your team members rise to the challenge? As we shall see later in this chapter, trust depends very much on the particular context – you can trust some people with some things in some situations, but not with other things or in other situations. In this chapter you'll learn what you can do to make it *safe* to trust others.

That's what I exist to do

Sometimes a belief is so deeply ingrained that it becomes a matter of identity. I was once working with a group of managers whose job roles had been changed as part of a restructuring. Their new role required them to be much more hands off – to let their staff take responsibility for all sorts of things on which the managers had previously had the final say. These managers were finding it difficult to let go, and I asked them why. Because that's what we exist to do, they replied. This is also a belief. People whose sense of identity is too closely wrapped up in their job role put themselves in a precarious position. At best they will find it difficult to move to a new job; at worst they are preparing for themselves a massive identity crisis when they retire – or are made redundant. Separating your beliefs from your sense of identity is well worth doing while you still have time.

I need to contribute

Consider this belief: I only really earn my keep if I shoulder all the responsibility for the work of my department. Carried to its logical conclusion, this means that you're not going to be very effective at sharing that responsibility with the rest of your team. But what underlies this belief is something very worthwhile – the need to contribute. So if making a contribution is important to you, can you still make a contribution when you trust people? Absolutely! You can contribute more to your company if you are able to develop in others the skills and sense of responsibility which you feel. This is better for your company, better for your team members and better for your long-term career prospects.

CHANGING BELIEFS

Beliefs can be difficult to shift. If your experience of working life has confirmed the validity of your beliefs over many years, then it might be difficult to change them quickly. But the world of work is changing rapidly, and your old beliefs may no longer serve you in the new workplace – in fact they can be a big disadvantage. It's worth asking yourself two questions:

● What beliefs do I currently hold about delegating and sharing responsibility?

● What beliefs might be more useful to me in the future?

John Dwyer at Leyland Trucks knows about changing beliefs. The name Leyland is often associated with failure in the British automotive industry, but from the ashes of the nationalized disaster have arisen a number of remarkable success stories. One of these is Leyland Trucks. Dwyer was originally recruited to the then publicly owned British Leyland because of his fearsome reputation at Ford's Halewood plant. He was a tough operator who would trust no one on the shopfloor. In fact, he was known as 'the rottweiler'. But as Leyland Trucks was sold off, first to the Dutch DAF group and then to a management buyout, Dwyer realized that his old beliefs were no longer appropriate. Trusting no one had made a lot of sense in the climate of hostile industrial relations which characterized much of the British automotive industry in the 1970s; it makes no sense at all in the climate of mutual trust which characterizes the highly successful Leyland Trucks in the 1990s. Dwyer shifted his beliefs so much that, as production director, he was a key figure in the development of the self-managed teams which make Leyland Trucks' production line so extraordinarily efficient.

HOW TO MAKE PEOPLE ACCOUNTABLE

We all want to be trusted, but we all find it hard to trust other people. Trusting others involves an element of risk – the nagging question of whether they will let us down. If you want to be skilful at making people accountable, you have to be good at assessing risk.

ASSESS THE RISK

As we saw previously, Jack Stack dramatically turned around SRC by giving the workforce a huge amount of responsibility, especially on the financial side of the business. But how did he begin? With a grand flourish and the announcement that all the company rules were to be put in the trash because henceforth management would completely trust the staff? No. When Stack first took over at SRC he judged that the workforce was too bitter and disillusioned to be trusted with too much responsibility –

SRC

it would simply be thrown back in his face. But he knew he had to do something which would begin to reverse the vicious cycle of mistrust which had existed in the company to date. Stack began by allowing staff to paint their own work areas:

> We had American flags, Hell's Angel insignia, everything you can imagine. There were signs and symbols everywhere, and none of it was colour co-ordinated. It looked awful, but it was theirs. When they brought their families in they could say, 'Here's where I work, this is my environment.' We also hoped that painting would encourage good housekeeping, which is important in a factory for reasons of both safety and efficiency.

Jack Stack took two factors into account when assessing the risk of trusting these people with this task:

- Their skills – are they able to do the task?
- Their attitudes and beliefs – are they committed to the task?

In the case of SRC, Stack knew that his people were able to do the task; whether they were willing to do it was an open question. Stack also assessed the consequences of the task not being done. There can be said to be two kinds of risk. There is above-the-waterline risk – if things go wrong, the consequences might be serious, but they will not jeopardize the success of the enterprise as a whole. And there is below-the-waterline risk: if a ship is holed below the waterline it sinks. Asking people to paint their working areas is clearly an above-the-waterline risk and well worth taking.

Monolithic Memories

When you start to trust people, start small, with above-the-waterline risks if you can. Sometimes, you don't have any option. The situation at semiconductor maker Monolithic Memories was a little different from that at SRC. In 1990 CEO Irwin Federman was facing a crisis. The company was on the verge of bankruptcy. As he told his staff:

If the top line ain't bigger than the middle, the bottom line will be red, and we have no margin for red any more. So either we fix it, or say what the hell and go out looking for new jobs full time now.

Federman wasn't sure about the skills of his staff, but he had a lot of faith in their commitment, especially in the face of so much risk and uncertainty. He asked his managers to come up with a plan, and told them that he trusted them to implement it. He increased everyone's purchasing authority by ten times and told them to get on with it. The result:

In four weeks we did a $660,000 profit turnaround, which included shipping about 40% more product, a level from which we have never retreated. Giving folks that kind of authority had a significant benefit in the self esteem department.

CLARIFY EXPECTATIONS

In relationships based on power, people are often given the haziest of instructions and expected to be a mind reader to find out what is really expected. This isn't terminal, because there will be plenty of checking and supervising along the way to guide the person back on course. But in relationships based on trust, you have to be very clear at the outset what you expect from the other person. Only then is it equitable to make them accountable.

There are five things you need to make very clear to the person you are trusting with a task. The word OPERA comes from the Latin *opera*, meaning work (hence operate), and so forms an appropriate acronym for the five steps. It is also pleasing that the *Oxford English Dictionary* begins its definition of the word opera with 'dramatic performance', which is exactly what you will get with this approach.

Outcomes

Outcomes. You need to let the other person know exactly what you expect of them, in terms which have a common meaning for both of you. One of the most common causes of communication breakdown is when people interpret the same words in different ways. As Benjamin Disraeli once wrote in a note to an aspiring author: 'Thank you so much for the book. I shall lose no time in reading it.' The trouble with the world of business is that it is full of words which are open to ambiguity. Put two businesspeople in a room and they will probably have different ideas of what constitutes:

- a good business plan

- an effective team

- a comprehensive marketing strategy

- a good report

and so on.

When you are discussing outcomes, don't assume that the other person thinks in the same way as you do. Discuss the desired outcome not just in abstract words like 'a good report', but in terms of things that you can see, hear and touch. A good question to keep asking at this stage is: 'How would we know that we've achieved this outcome?'

Parameters. What you don't want to do is to spell out every detail of the method you want to the person to use in achieving this outcome. If you do, you are reverting to a power-based relationship and the person won't truly feel accountable. On the other hand, it is not right to conceal from them the basic dos and don'ts associated with the task. In other words, you need to give them the broad parameters within which they should operate – some guidelines, if you like. In particular, are there any values you would wish to bring to their attention?

Effects. What are the effects, or consequences, of achieving or not achieving the task? Both you and the other person need to have a clear, shared view of both the benefits of getting it right and the risks of getting it wrong. This is where you tell them the score – explain how their

Parameters

Effects

individual actions will contribute to the big picture. It's often at this point that you begin to get an idea of how committed the person will be to the task.

Resources. What resources are available to the person to do the job – physical, financial, human, time? In many organizations the most precious resource is time and the biggest favour you can do the other person is freeing up some time for them to do the task. If you are not confident that the person has the resources to do the job, then you are setting them up to fail.

Resources

Accountability. The final step is crucial: you need to make it clear that the other person will be accountable for the task. You do this by agreeing with them how, when and where they will be asked to account for what they have done. There is an important point to underline here: you are holding them accountable for their *results*, not their *methods*. How they do the task (within the parameters you have outlined) is up to them.

Accountability

This approach is undoubtedly tough on other people because you really are holding them accountable for what they do – and this means facing the consequences of success or failure. But sharing responsibility means being tough on yourself too, because it involves the thing many managers find hardest of all – letting go. Constantly looking over someone's shoulder will not only harm trust, but it can knock the person's confidence to the extent that they may well turn in a worse job than if you had left them to it. You can probably get away with a friendly 'How's it going then?', but as soon as you start asking whether they will be keeping to the deadline, or criticizing what you have heard on the grapevine about their approach, you destroy the trust. You should certainly make yourself available if the other person requests it, but you should not interfere otherwise. What about a really major project – do you have to wait to the very end to discover that it has all gone wrong? Of course not. You build in review meetings as part of the accountability stage of clarifying the task. But these meetings should be agreed at the very outset of the project, not imposed unilaterally when you

Letting go

lose your nerve and wonder whether you can really trust the person. Putting time in up front enables you to develop trust more effectively later on.

RESPOND TO RESULTS

So you've taken all this trouble to share responsibility effectively – you've overcome your initial resistance, assessed the risk, clarified the task and made the other person accountable. What happens next? If the other person has completed the task to the standards you asked for it is easy – you thank them, ask them to share what they have learned with you and others, and revise upwards your assessment of their competence. But if they have failed, either partially or completely, then your trust in them has been violated.

Your response should depend on the circumstances and the other person's response to their failure. If the circumstances indicate that the failure was really outside the person's control, and they offer some recompense, then you should be forgiving. On the other hand, if failure appears to be the other person's responsibility but they won't accept it, then you need to respond in a tough and robust way; especially if this is not the first time you've been let down. If it is a colleague, you won't be asking them again in a hurry; if it's a supplier or partner you should consider seriously ending the relationship. You will engender the trust of the trustworthy only if you respond with vigour to those who are untrustworthy. Most lapses of trust are seldom clear cut; by assessing the relative weight of the two factors you can come to a decision as to how to go forward.

HOW FAR CAN YOU GO?

Once an organization realizes that making people accountable works it can produce extraordinary results.

Large and successful companies sometimes find themselves with quite substantial sums of cash which they don't need immediately. Rather than leaving it in their bank account, they tend to invest it in a way which gives them a high rate of interest without committing the money for too long. This is often referred to as the treasury function and it is traditionally carried out by the company's most senior financial officers. If you haven't heard of this process before, that's because it is usually a well-guarded secret. The company's financial guardians usually take the view that if the workforce knew there was this extra cash sloshing around, they would be demanding wage increases and so on.

Power generation company AES takes a different view. The company asked for volunteers to handle the treasury function for a while, and a maintenance team at an AES plant in Connecticut said they were interested. Maintenance technician Leo Bernstein explains:

> We were a little apprehensive at first. The company had given us $8.2 million to invest and not many companies trust maintenance technicians with that kind of money. Well, the finance department gave us a little course and trained us pretty well. We started calling up investment houses to see what they could offer and after a while we started really having fun. We were all egging each other on to see who could get the best rates.

AES explores other ways of making people accountable. One issue on which everyone is agreed is the need to stamp out the 'us and them' culture which pervades many organizations. Each year, senior officers of the company spend a week at a specific operating plant, doing whatever jobs the plant operators tell them to do. Although the plants are highly automated, in the power generation industry there are still plenty of hot, wet and dirty jobs to be done. As well as having a symbolic value, this also allows executives to find out plant operators' current concerns.

AES continually experiments with more decentralization – devolving functions and responsibilities which traditional companies would keep at corporate headquarters.

Budgeting is one example of this. Teams set their own budgets, and this leads to a real ownership of financial matters. One day, a plant technician was doing the family shopping when he noticed some $24 fans for sale. These were identical to the fans which were used in the plant where he worked, but he knew the company was paying $75 each, and that they wore out pretty quickly because of the working atmosphere. So he took out his personal credit card and bought the entire stock in the store.

In this example, the fans were exactly right; there have been examples where other employees have done something similar but got it wrong. In one case someone purchased a useless air heater costing $10,000. But the company applauds this initiative too – it wants staff who feel committed, not those who live in fear of being punished for making mistakes. The company now has a market value of $2 billion, and was recently ranked 58 on *Fortune*'s list of America's 100 fastest growing companies.

MAKING EVERYONE ACCOUNTABLE

Making staff in your own team or department accountable is one thing – how do you go about changing the culture of an entire organization? The same steps apply.

Training

When David Green took over as chief executive of the international development agency Voluntary Service Overseas (VSO), he knew that he had to change the prevailing culture of the organization, where all decisions had to be made at the very top. But he also knew that Irwin Federman's approach at Monolithic Memories – simply upping managers' authority – wouldn't work. Senior staff at VSO were so used to passing the buck upwards that their ability to take responsibility for big decisions had simply wasted away. VSO commissioned a big training programme in decision making and teamwork, initially for managers and later for all VSO staff. This training equipped staff with the skills and confidence to create the kind of climate for taking responsibility which Green wanted. You will recall that AES didn't simply let its maintenance technicians loose on $9 million dollars – it trained them first.

Training clearly helps with skills, but what about commitment? Sad to say, training probably won't help here – in fact, sending unwilling conscripts to be trained will probably make matters worse. If someone is going to be committed to taking on more responsibility, they'll want an answer to the question: 'What's in it for me?' Different people will be looking for different answers. For some, the inherent satisfaction of the work may be its own reward. For others, the opportunity to develop new skills may be the prime motivator. For yet others, financial rewards may be part of the motivation.

Commitment

Clarifying expectations is another crucial step in creating accountability in the high trust organization. If staff are to take responsibility, they need to understand how their actions contribute to the success of the business as a whole. They need to appreciate the ins and outs of the business at least as well as its owners might. That's why telling people the score is so important.

Clarifying expectations

Obviously, people need to receive feedback on whether they've done the right thing or not. Good, straight, honest feedback is a bit of a rarity in many organizations; in Chapter 9 we'll see why this is so and what you can do about it. People also need to know that if they cannot produce results, then the relationship of trust will end – and in some cases this means leaving the organization.

Respond to results

BETTER SYSTEMS, MORE TRUST

We've looked at the beliefs and skills you need to be able to make people accountable for what they do. But what about the influence of the organizational environment, and in particular, what about systems and structures?

Back in 1962 Procter & Gamble was celebrating its 125th birthday and was a tremendously successful company. Nevertheless, one or two senior P&G people were wondering whether it was really worth measuring,

Procter & Gamble

sometimes to half a second, how long it took someone to climb a ladder or stir a vat, so that it could be incorporated into the company's gargantuan rulebook. They called in management consultant Douglas McGregor who helped them set up a new plant in Augusta, Georgia. P&G's formal rulebook and hierarchy were both abandoned – everyone worked in teams, setting their own goals and sharing out the work. The plant was such a success that henceforth every new P&G plant was built on the same lines, culminating in what was described as the best industrial plant in the United States – P&G's Lima, Ohio plant. Instead of monitoring methods, staff were held accountable for their results – and the results were good. Production costs were half that of a conventional plant and wages correspondingly high.

One of the most visible aspects of high trust organizations is their lack of bureaucracy. Nordstrom, as we have seen, relies on a one-line employee handbook which enjoins staff to trust their own best judgement at all times. The organization which has gone the furthest in this respect is WL Gore and Associates. The company has no formal structure, no job titles and almost nothing in the way of systems and procedures. Gore associates are asked to follow four guiding principles: try to be fair; use your freedom to grow; make your commitments and keep them; consult with other associates prior to any action that may adversely affect the reputation or financial stability of the company. Apart from that, the company has no other policies. And yet it has grown from sales of $6 million in 1969 to $660 million in 1990. This tremendous growth has been financed almost entirely without debt.

In his book *Maverick*, Semco CEO Ricardo Semler describes his philosophy on company rules:

WL Gore

Semco

> One of my first acts at Semco was to throw out the rules. All companies have procedural bibles. Some look like the *Encyclopaedia Britannica*. Who needs all those rules? They discourage flexibility and comfort the complacent. At Semco, we stay away from formulas and

try to keep our minds open. I knew the rule book was useless when, as a test, I once distributed some additional pages for it. I asked some managers to read the new sections and give me their reactions. Almost everyone said they were just fine. Trouble was, I had stapled the pages together so that they couldn't be read without first prying them apart. Funny how no one mentioned that. All that new employees get today is a 20 page booklet, which has lots of cartoons but few words. The basic message: use your common sense.

Do organizations achieve high levels of trust because they don't have bureaucratic rules; or do they do without bureaucratic rules because they have high levels of trust? The answer is yes – both are true. This raises the obvious question: if you currently suffer from low levels of trust in your organization and massive bureaucracy, how can you begin to change things? Assess the risk of changing or scrapping the rules. Clarify expectations. Respond to results.

To see how this works in practice, let's look at the case of Leyland Trucks. An important source of success has been the company's ability to cut away bureaucracy and systems which diminish trust. It used to have a big problem with kettles in the assembly area. There's an obvious safety risk in having a small, free-standing object full of boiling water in an area where very heavy pieces of machinery are being lifted and manipulated. Staff were told that they had to use the vending machines, and every so often there was a purge on kettles. The kettle ban, and the regular purges, did nothing for management–staff relations. As one worker put it: 'My wife trusts me to use a kettle at home, but you don't trust me to make myself a cup of coffee at work.' The mistrust was exacerbated by the fact that office staff did have kettles and could drink as much tea and coffee as they wanted. The solution – provide safe, fixed boilers which meet the safety requirements and allow shopfloor workers to brew up as often as they want.

Leyland Trucks

This example sounds trivial, and yet it is often the small things which make a big difference to trust, partly because they are often symbols of something much bigger. In this case the kettle issue symbolized the difference between shopfloor staff and office workers. Many organizational systems enshrine this difference – there was once a time when some British manufacturers had as many as five different canteens on the same site to reflect the status needs of unskilled workers, semi-skilled workers, office staff, managers and senior executives. Those days are fortunately gone for ever, and high trust organizations generally have single-status terms and conditions for all staff.

To take the example of Leyland Trucks again, at one time managers had to approve the expenditure on every new tool. The absurdity of this was brought home to production director Dwyer when a worker came to him and said: 'How much does a replacement for this spanner cost?' '£2.79,' he replied. 'Wrong,' said the worker. 'It costs £8.79: £2.79 for the spanner and £6 which the company has paid me for the time I've taken to find you to get approval.' Following this episode, the workforce was asked for ways of improving this situation and it was agreed to make the shopfloor teams responsible for their own tool budgets. The accountability is still there – if the team overruns its annual budget for tools serious questions will be asked. But by trusting the workers, and checking infrequently, the cost of tools actually dropped by 30 per cent in the first year of operating the new system.

In both cases, the petty rules were done away with. More importantly, the accountability was put where it belonged, in a way which made sense to the people involved. Having a high trust organization isn't about having no accountability – **it's about having the accountability in the right place**. Begin small, by abolishing petty rules. Then move up to things like equipment budgets. Then keep rolling until you achieve the level of shared responsibility which AES achieves.

Hewlett-Packard co-founder Dave Packard reflected on an experience which was to be influential in the way he later went on to run his company:

An early lesson in trust

> I learned, early in my career, some of the problems that can be caused by a company's lack of trust in its people. In the late 1930s, when I was working for General Electric in Schenectady, the company was making a big thing of plant security. I'm sure others were too. GE was especially zealous about guarding its tool and parts bins to make sure employees didn't steal anything. Faced with this obvious display of mistrust, many employees set out to prove it justified, walking off with tools or parts whenever they could. Eventually, GE tools and parts were scattered all around the town, including the attic of the house in which a number of us were living. In fact, we had so much equipment up there that when we threw the switch, the lights on the entire street would dim.
>
> The irony of all this is that many of the tools and parts were being used by their GE 'owners' to work on either job-related projects or skill-enhancing hobbies – activities that would likely improve their performance on the job.

MAKING SUPPLIERS ACCOUNTABLE

So far in this chapter we've put the spotlight on organizations sharing responsibility with their employees. Even greater benefits are possible when companies share responsibility with their suppliers. According to Nirmalya Kumar, professor of marketing at the International Institute for Management Development in Lausanne, Switzerland:

> A crucial question is whether powerful manufacturers or retailers receive more tangible benefits from building trusting relationships with partners than from exploiting their clout. Is trust more than a feel good phenomenon?

The results [of a survey of 1500 manufacturer–retailer relationships] show that retailers with a high level of trust in the manufacturer generated 78% more sales than those with a low level.

Marks & Spencer

One of the world's experts at developing high trust relationships with suppliers is Marks & Spencer. M&S endeavours to identify what its customers really want and to deliver that reliably. M&S's own label, St Michael, is synonymous with quality for many British shoppers. In order to achieve quality and reliability, the company has to be able to plan production over the short, medium and long term. So far as M&S is concerned, the only way to do this is by establishing a relationship of trust with its suppliers. Such relationships are not achieved overnight but, once established, are a great source of competitive advantage. From the retailer's point of view, you can rely on the quality and delivery of products over time. From the supplier's point of view, a committed and close long-term relationship makes it easier to smooth out the peaks and troughs in production and plan for long-term investment.

What makes for a good relationship with suppliers? Former M&S deputy chairman Brian Howard:

Personal relationships between the two organizations have to be very close indeed, at all levels – day to day management, executive and board level. It's often assumed that if people are too close a certain amount of 'softness' will creep in. I have never found that personal relationships lead to an abuse of position. There is as much cut and thrust as you can imagine there ought to be between any supplier and retailer. But it is quite acceptable for both sides to negotiate hard because they are both on the same wavelength – there is trust and fairness of everyone involved. You also can't have trust unless you're willing to share information. M&S has always been very open with the real figures to its suppliers. Building trust requires a lot of skill and application.

In other words, M&S makes sure that with its suppliers it clarifies expectations and responds to results. The more customers expect flexibility and innovation on the part of the retailer, and the more new technology is able to provide a tightly integrated supply chain from manufacturer to customer, the more important high trust relationships between all the parties involved become. While many US firms have taken the lead in developing trust *within* the company, British firms like M&S have generally been in the forefront of developing high trust relationships with suppliers as well. Partly this is a result of a cultural difference between US and UK retailers. In the US, the manufacturer's brand tends to be pre-eminent; in the UK, the retailer's own label is often of more importance, as M&S demonstrates. Nevertheless, North American companies are beginning to see the value of closer ties with suppliers.

At the end of the 1980s Chrysler was generally considered the poor relation of the American auto industry – certainly it was well behind both GM and Ford in terms of profitability. By 1994 the situation had completely changed and Chrysler is now more profitable than both of its major rivals. Chrysler's president Robert Lutz attributes this achievement almost entirely to a policy of greater trust towards suppliers, based on openness. Like most American automakers, Chrysler had traditionally taken a very adversarial and secretive attitude to its suppliers, with one thing in mind – to drive down costs. But this approach resulted in the opposite: the transaction costs of setting so many suppliers against each other, and problems with quality, sent costs rocketing. When Lutz took over in 1988 he set out to create the kind of close, trusting, long-term relationships with suppliers which are more associated with the Japanese.

Chrysler

At the heart of this was the SCORE programme. Launched by Lutz in 1989, the aim of the Supplier Cost Reduction Effort was to identify ways of reducing costs at both Chrysler and its suppliers – with both parties sharing the benefits. Lutz's message was: 'I want your brainpower, not your margins'. Implementing SCORE required an unparallelled level of openness on both sides, and a close working relationship which was unprecedented in the industry. In fact, at the very time Chrysler was encouraging its buyers to take suppliers out to lunch, GM was forbidding its buyers to accept lunch invitations from suppliers. By 1996, the SCORE programme had led to the implementation of 5300 cost-saving ideas, saving Chrysler $1.7 billion a year. Profit per vehicle increased from $250 in the early 1980s to $2110 in the mid-1990s.

THE MILLIPEDE

When a large manufacturer can choose between many small suppliers, it sometimes seems that the balance of power is one sided. However much a small supplier may want to raise the level of trust in its relationship with a large manufacturer, it is dependent on a more powerful partner being willing to play ball. At least this is how it seems in the short term.

Airedale Springs Ltd chairman Michael Parkinson puts this into perspective:

'All the big names in British industry are supported by little suppliers like us. And if they drive a few of us out of business, they don't seem to mind too much. A millipede doesn't notice if it loses a few legs. But if it goes on being careless with its legs it suddenly finds one day that the body cannot move. The same is true of the big names in industry – if they carry on being too ruthless with their suppliers they will find themselves one day like the legless millipede.'

Identify Their Concerns 6

Management has to have credibility. Without it, people won't listen to you. There must be a level of mutual respect and trust. People have to feel that, whatever your faults, you have some sensitivity to them and their problems, you value their contributions, you'll offer them a fair shake. At the very least, they have to be willing to give you the benefit of the doubt.

Jack Stack, CEO, SRC

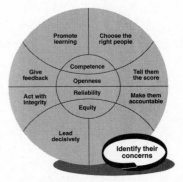

*T*HE fourth principle of at the CORE of the trust effect is equity – fairness. One of the quickest ways to sow the seeds of mistrust in a team is to treat team members unfairly. Choose one or two favourites and give them all the interesting jobs, the best computers, the most comfortable desks. Overlook their major foul-ups, and instead nit pick over trivial errors made by other team members. If you really want to rub salt into the wound, make sure that one of your team members is performing abysmally, and do nothing about it – except maybe force other team members to cover up for him or her. Have you ever been a member of a team with a boss who acted unfairly in this way? Then you will know how deeply destructive of trust it is. Would you ever act like the team leader of this mythical team? Of course not. But this poses a dilemma – almost everyone has some experience of being treated in this way, but no one ever admits to doing it themselves. What's going on? The answer is, of course, that people who act in this way are often unaware that they are acting unfairly.

Self-fulfilling prophecies

If you give the interesting jobs and the best resources to some people and not to others, you may not consider this inequitable at all – you may reason that you simply favour those who deserve it. And you may be right. Or you may be succumbing to a self-fulfilling prophecy. In a famous social psychology experiment, Robert Rosenthal and Lenore Jacobson gave the pupils of an American elementary school an intelligence test. They then chose 20 per cent of the children at random, and told the teachers that the test had shown these children to be capable of significant academic progress. No further action was taken until the pupils took a similar intelligence test a year later. The 20 per cent who had been identified as capable of progress were not only well ahead of their classmates in reading and maths, they had gained an average of 15 IQ points more than their contemporaries. Simply believing a thing can make it so. That is why first impressions are often correct – we make them so.

The consequences of this research for business are rather serious. If, for whatever reason, you begin to treat a particular team member as if she is an especially good worker, she will become more effective. If you treat another team member as if he is no good, he will become less effective.

So how do you know whether your treatment of staff is good judgement of competence and commitment, or merely a self-fulfilling prophecy? In a sense it doesn't much matter. What does matter very much is how each team member responds to the way you treat them and their colleagues. To find this out you need to identify your people's concerns.

Apart from the dangers of the self-fulfilling prophecy, there is another reason that equity is hard to achieve: different people may value different things. As we saw in the Volkswagen example in Chapter 2, managers assumed that staff valued wage rises more than changed working practices. In reality, the opposite was true. If you are going to be able to treat people fairly, you need to find out what their real concerns are – not what concerns you think they ought to have. And to do all this you have to **listen**.

Valuing different things

Identifying concerns is an essential part of trust. It is also an essential component of leadership. You are able to lead only if others are willing to follow; and other people will follow your lead only if they believe that you share their concerns – in other words, if you have their best interests at heart. You can only do this if you know what their concerns are, and you can only do this if you ask them – and listen carefully to what they have to say.

Listening

In many organizations, managers don't spend much time listening. When Dennis Longstreet became president of a company in the Johnson & Johnson group, he realized that the thing he had to work on most to establish credibility was his listening skills:

I think that most management, particularly white male management, has a tendency to listen for about ten seconds and then solve the problem. That's the way I was trained, that's the way I moved through the organization, and so I would attempt to fix problems quickly. That's not necessarily a style that works.

Certainly in many European and North American organizations, managers like to be seen talking and doing, not listening or thinking. But as Longstreet says, that's not always the best way. In fact, one of the strongest signs that a company is in terminal decline is the unwillingness of its senior managers to listen. Neither Robert Maxwell, who apparently committed suicide after failing to prop up his newspaper empire with money diverted from its staff pension fund, nor junk bond king Michael Milken, who ended up in prison for his part in the destruction of Drexel Burnham Lambert, had much of a reputation for being good listeners. Talkers, yes, but listeners, no. Listening is an alien activity to many managers, but it has great merit – especially in building trust.

HOW TO IDENTIFY CONCERNS

SET QUANTITATIVE LISTENING GOALS

How important do you think it is to listen? Most people will tell you that they think it is very important, but their actions tell a different story. If you dig deep enough, many people hold a belief that listening is not 'real work'. In many Western male managers, there's an in-built belief that real work is about doing, not listening. But if you look at the people who reach the top job in high performance, high trust organizations, they spend a lot of time listening.

Sam Walton used to spend most of his time in his Wal-Mart stores, chatting to staff and customers, working the floor, helping the clerks. He regularly used to ride on the delivery trucks and listen to what his drivers had to say about the company. Each generation of Nordstrom bosses, from founder John Nordstrom to brothers Bruce, Jim and John who now make up the chairman's office, has spent a great deal of time on the sales floor, listening to customers and associates. It's part of the Nordstrom ethos that you learn the business literally and figuratively kneeling in front of the customer. Hewlett-Packard has also institutionalized listening in the form of what it calls MBWA: management by walking around.

Because listening is important, but not always urgent, its easy to put it off until you have more time – which means you may never do it. If something is important, it is worth measuring your success at doing it. So set yourself a quantitative goal for the amount of time you will devote to listening to your constituents. Senior managers of UK building society Birmingham Midshires have job descriptions which require them to spend at least 60 per cent of their time not at headquarters but out in the branches – thus setting a numerical goal for the amount of time spent listening to their key constituents, staff and customers.

If you really want to know what someone thinks, it's best to meet at their place, not yours. That's why many successful chief executives spend so much of their time 'on the road' – meeting staff, customers, suppliers, partners. An especially effective way of getting at employees' real concerns is to work alongside them. Pete Blackmore, general manager of the Florence, Kentucky distribution centre of Levi Strauss & Co, regularly spends a day on the plant floor packing jeans and carting boxes around – and encourages fellow managers to do the same.

CHOOSE THE RIGHT SETTING

Telephone bank First Direct's former chief executive Kevin Newman made a point of meeting with all of the organization's 2000 staff, at least once a year, for two or three hours. Some years this was in groups of only 20 or so, sometimes in groups of 50 or 60. It was important that the dialogue is two way and open. Newman commented:

> In some of these sessions I get quite charged up and start to show quite a bit of emotion – but I think that's OK. If you display your vulnerability and admit mistakes the vast majority of people will repay your openness. You can't demand trust – you have to earn it.

Some senior managers have forgone offices altogether. Birmingham Midshires chief Michael Jackson argues that he spends so much of his time on the road that he doesn't need an office at all. When he is at HQ, he finds a space to work in the open-plan offices alongside everyone else.

Do you need an office?

Other structures can help – Leyland Trucks has 'meet the manager' sessions where senior managers regularly spend time down on the shopfloor talking with assembly line workers. Many high trust organizations organize social events where employees can get together. Hewlett-Packard first began its company picnics back in the 1950s, when the company had just 200 employees. Well into the

Social events

1960s co-founders Dave Packard and Bill Hewlett would serve up the food and chat to associates and their families. Now that the company employs over 90,000 people the tradition of company picnics continues at HP sites all over the world and senior staff take their turns at serving up the food.

Face-to-face meetings are important

As the technologies of videophones and e-mail become more commonplace, will face-to-face meetings become redundant? Certainly, new technologies will make a big difference in the transmission of facts and figures, and can also help to maintain a well-established relationship of trust; but trust cannot be created through electronic media. The only way to develop trust with someone is to meet them face to face.

When David Blunkett took over as Secretary of State for Education after Labour's win in the 1997 British general election, he realized that he needed to win credibility with his team of more than 2000 civil servants at the Department for Education. He needed to do this fast if he was to begin to redeem Labour's election pledge of making education its top priority. Blunkett invited the whole department to a meeting at Central Hall, Westminster. For the first time on record, a Secretary of State addressed his entire staff face to face. As they arrived at the meeting, many were cynical that this was nothing more than a public relations gimmick. But when they left an hour later, most had been won over. What had convinced them was the fact that Blunkett and his ministers had been willing to answer some awkward questions from rank-and-file civil servants. The exaggerated respect and protocol which used to get in the way of honest working relationships seemed to have been swept away.

This isn't to say that such big events are the only way for senior managers to make contact with and listen to their staff, but they do play a part. And the face-to-face aspect is important. Chief executives who believe they can win the trust of their staff by broadcasting hearty messages over the company's in-house video channel are barking up the wrong tree: there's no substitute for personal contact. Organizations which thrive as 'virtual organizations' – corporations without offices which exist as a network of home- or car-based workers – realize this. They make specific opportunities to meet, in the form of training, staff conferences and social events. What these meetings do is provide an opportunity to share concerns and build trust.

In Chapter 3 we saw how important perceptive listening was to the business of choosing the right people. We looked at the four elements of perceptive listening – rapport, pushing for specifics, drawing conclusions and looking for consistency. How are these elements relevant to the business of listening to staff, customers and suppliers?

LISTEN PERCEPTIVELY

Rapport is the ability to perceive the world as others perceive it, so that you can communicate with them better. Noticing their energy level, posture and gesture is one way of doing this. Another way is to notice not just the individual words, but the kind of language patterns they use. In particular, do they tend to talk in generalities, are they interested in 'the big picture'? Or are they more concerned with the specifics, the small details? Whichever they are – and both are equally useful ways of perceiving the world – you will communicate with them better if you notice their preference and do the same.

Rapport

A very common form of communication breakdown occurs when senior managers want to talk about company strategy, end-of-year profits and the need for investment – the big picture – while staff want to know exactly what this year's bonus payment will be and when the canteen is going to be redecorated – the small details. The staff think the management are evasive wafflers and the managers think the staff are obsessed with trivia. Trust doesn't get much of a look in. Are you big picture or small detail? Have you got the flexibility to change if you meet people who are different?

At a selection interview, you know what you are looking for and the primary purpose of the interview – from your perspective anyway – is to find out if the candidate fits the

Push for specifics

bill. When you are identifying the concerns of staff, customers or others, the situation is different. You need to find out what the other person wants and how they would know when they've got it. So if a member of staff says that she wants better working conditions, don't just nod appreciatively and move the conversation on. Ask: what specifically would better working conditions be like? How would you know that working conditions were better? Likewise, when a supplier lets you know that he thinks communication between your company and his is poor, probe him to find out what he means by that. Pushing for details will come naturally to people who tend to focus on small details – but big picture people will find it harder.

Draw conclusions

Once you've amassed the detail you need, it's time to ask the question: and what would that do for you? Ask it again and again, until you begin to get an idea of the things which the other person values as fundamental. This may be the first time that the other person has put those feelings into words. Leaders who win the highest levels of trust do so by identifying not just what their people want, but what at some deeper level they really need.

An interesting feature of many high trust organizations is that they have achieved market success with products for which, initially at least, there was absolutely no demand. Think of 3M and Post-it notes, or Sony and the Walkman. Coincidence? Maybe. Or perhaps high trust companies are so good at listening that they are able to get beyond superficial wants to understanding as yet unperceived needs.

Look for consistency

A good example of inconsistency is when somebody responds to 'How are you?' with 'Just fine' – said in a dour tone of voice and accompanied with a sullen look, averted eyes and slouched shoulders. Of course, people are not usually this blatant, but in all kinds of other, more subtle ways, people show an inconsistency between what they say and how they say it. This is worth noticing and asking about. So get curious.

In the classic 1960s TV police serial *Dragnet*, Sgt Friday was fond of saying: 'Just give me the facts ma'am, just the facts.' It's all too easy to approach listening to your people with the same degree of impatience: tell me what I need to know so I can get back to work and sort it out. Quick fixes are seldom long lasting. Ask questions which might take you further into understanding what the person is really bothered about. Unearth the idea they have, but which they are too shy to thrust in your face.

This approach is particularly important if you haven't really listened much to this person before, or where your company culture doesn't promote straight, honest communication. Most managers think of themselves as fairly approachable and easy to talk to – the sort of person whom their staff would find it easy to be honest with. But many team members don't see their bosses like that at all. Most people think very carefully about what they would and wouldn't say to their immediate boss, and extremely carefully about what they would say to anyone more senior. So, if you are a senior manager, you are going to have to work hard to make it possible for people to be honest with you. Looking for consistency is one way to check that they are telling you the whole story. If you think there is more to be said, make it easy for the person to say it.

LISTENING AND TALKING ACROSS CULTURES

One of the reasons that trust is perceived differently by people of different national or ethnic backgrounds is the different ways we communicate – and that's even when we are talking the same language.

Consider the simple matter of the pause we leave between words. People brought up on the east coast of America tend to leave shorter gaps than those brought up in the south. So if Sally from Texas is in conversation with Bob from New York, she may find it difficult to get a word in edgeways. While she is waiting for a slight pause to begin, Bob has already started up again. And Bob can't understand why Sally seems to have nothing to say. In many Latin countries, the pause isn't there at all – it shows that you are interested in what someone else is saying if you make your response before they have finished speaking. At the other end of the scale, in many Oriental countries, long pauses occur between one person finishing a sentence and another beginning. This shows that you are interested in what they are saying because you have given enough time to listen and momentarily reflect on it. For many Westerners, the long pauses in conversations with a Japanese person can be disconcerting – unless you understand the reasons.

Likewise, body language has different meanings in different cultures. Maintaining eye contact can, in different cultures, be interpreted as a sign of polite interest, as a mark of insolence or even as an expression of sexual interest. If you want to establish rapport and trust with a business colleague in another country, it's worth checking how various gestures might be interpreted.

LISTENING TO CUSTOMERS

High trust organizations know how important it is to listen to customers. Like most other companies they conduct customer satisfaction surveys by phone, mail and face to face; and they encourage customer feedback through comment cards and helplines. What marks out high trust companies is the emphasis they put on the role of front-line staff, both to take the time to listen to customers and to have the responsibility to act on what they hear. Nordstrom sales associate Joyce Johnson is on first-name terms with most of her customers in the Corte Madera, California store:

> Whether you're in retail, real estate, banking or law, the idea is to listen to your customer. We go into the dressing room, have a sparkling water, and just yak about anything – the kids, the vacation. By the time we get to the merchandise, they're comfortable.

Her colleague Patrice Magasawa agrees:

The day I stopped worrying about selling and started listening to customers was the day it all fell into place for me. When you are young and starting out with this company, you want to sell. But the more you talk, and the less you listen, the less you're going to do.

If listening to customers is good at building trust and business, failing to listen can be catastrophic. In October 1994, Thomas Nicely, a maths professor at Lynchburg College in Virginia, posted a notice on the Internet describing a flaw in the way Intel's newly released Pentium chip did division. No only did Intel fail to listen to this customer's real concerns, it tried to deny them. Intel CEO Andy Grove promptly responded by posting a message to the effect that the flaw was so trivial that it would make no difference at all to most Pentium users. Technically, this was true; so far as Intel was concerned, this was true; so far as Intel's customers were concerned, they were being fobbed off.

The story was picked up by CNN which portrayed it as a serious problem. Jokes began to circulate in the computer community. Q: what's another name for the Intel Inside sticker they put on computers? A: the warning label. Computer users quickly lost trust in Intel and its new chip, and IBM halted shipment of all Pentium-based computers. Although Intel continued to argue that the chances of a faulty calculation occurring were so small as to be negligible, the public perception was that Intel's chips were no longer reliable. Intel stalled a little longer, but it was eventually forced to offer a full, no questions asked, replacement policy. The flawed Pentiums were sold to a jewellery company for use as earrings and Intel suffered a write down in stock value of $475 million.

LISTENING TO OTHER STAKEHOLDERS

Many organizations already recognize the importance of listening to staff and of listening to customers. But only more recently has the importance of listening to other stakeholders started to move up the corporate agenda. Cor Herkströter is group managing director of Royal Dutch/Shell, one of the largest and most profitable industrial enterprises in the world. He recently addressed these issues in a speech in Amsterdam:

> Development, especially in the way people communicate and obtain information, has changed many aspects of our lives. Most of these changes have been positive. We now have more choice and more information than ever before. However, there have also been negative effects – one being a widespread loss of trust in many of our established institutions and ideologies. At the same time, and perhaps paradoxically, these developments have led to expanded expectations being placed on other organizations – including multinational companies.
>
> From our point of view as a major multinational, these expanded expectations often seen contradictory – one group wants us to do one thing, while another expects something else altogether. A good example was the Brent Spar. We went through a three year process of identifying the best environmental option for the disposal of this unique structure. This identified deep sea disposal as the best option. We tested this preferred solution with British environmentalists and scientists. It satisfied all the appropriate regulations and was approved by the UK Government. But, we found out that what appeared to be the best option in the UK was not acceptable elsewhere. We were caught between two different approaches to the environment. The public reacted in a way that we did not expect and the pressure groups used the Spar as a symbol in a way we did not anticipate.

A campaign led by the environmental group Greenpeace resulted in many European motorists refusing to use Shell petrol and this had a financial impact even on the huge Shell group. The company's reputation was severely tarnished, and it eventually bowed to pressure and changed its mind about the disposal of the Spar. How could a large and sophisticated company like Shell get it so wrong? Cor Herkströter again:

> Naturally we have listened to our customers. We have listened very closely to governments and our staff. Of course we also dealt with environmentalist groups, consumer groups and so on, but we tended to let the public affairs department deal with them. They were important, but they were not as important as government, industry organizations and so on. In essence, we were slow in understanding that these groups were acquiring authority. Meanwhile, those institutions we were used to dealing with, were tending to lose authority. One major reason, from my perspective, was a type of technological arrogance which is rather common in companies with a strong technical base. For most engineering problems there is a correct answer. For most social and political dilemmas there is a range of possible answers – almost all compromises.

Companies cannot make informed decisions about the relative demands of all their stakeholders – in other words they cannot identify their concerns and act equitably – unless they make a real attempt to listen to the needs and wants of the different stakeholder groups. And it cannot be assumed that all members of a common group want the same thing. Moreover, as Shell realized, the relative authority of these groups may change over time. Listening carefully to stakeholders is essential for organizations in maintaining their reputation.

THE EFFECT OF LISTENING

To make sure that employees were able to have a strong voice in the running of the company, in 1990 coffee company Starbucks set up a number of project teams made up of workers from across the company. One of these was the 'people growth' team, which, among other things, recommended that the company implement a stock option plan. But there were other effects too, as Howard Schultz reports:

'How do you measure the benefits of listening to your people and sharing ownership with them? You can't. But the benefits can run deeper than you think. One member of the "people growth" team was Martin Shaughnessy, a tall, talkative, pony-tailed man who worked in receiving, unloading the heavy burlap bags of green coffee at the plant. He was amazed and thrilled to be invited to offsite meetings with office workers, asked for his input, and given the opportunity to present ideas to management. Months later he came into my office and told me we needed a professional distribution manager – in effect, asking us to hire him a boss. I asked him to write up a proposal and make a presentation to the executive board. He did, and within six months we acted on his proposal.

One day in 1992, Martin came into the human resources department bearing a letter, signed by an overwhelming majority of the warehouse and roasting plant employees, indicating that they no longer wished to be represented by the union. "You included us in the running of this business," he said. "When we complained, you fixed the problem. You trusted us, and now we trust you." '

Lead Decisively 7

I may not come up with brilliant ideas, but I'm good at crystallizing and synthesizing the ideas of others – I think this is a more engaging form of leadership.

> Peter Hewitt, chief executive, Northern Arts

I try very hard to avoid making decisions – my job is to enable and equip other people to make decisions.

> Kevin Newman, former chief executive, First Direct

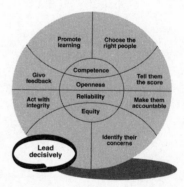

*I*F you want to create relationships based on trust, then you have to listen to people to identify their concerns. But listening in itself is not enough. You also have to **lead**. This chapter is about one crucial aspect of leadership – the way in which people make decisions. But the focus of this chapter is not on making the 'right' decision. In the complex world of business, you sometimes never know whether a decision was the right one or not. What this chapter is about is **making decisions the right way** – in a way which engenders trust.

Psychologists who have studied the subject of equity identify two forms of justice. Distributive justice relates to outcomes – who gets what. Procedural justice is concerned with the way in which decisions are reached – the process which leads to the final distribution. Both are important, but procedural justice is the one people are most bothered about. You'll recall the cases of Algoma Steel and VW's Mexico plant in Chapter 2. In both cases, trust in the management centred not on the final outcome, but on the way in which the decision was reached. In both cases, the managers initially failed to consult directly with the people affected.

Does this mean that consultation is always the best way to make a decision? Unfortunately, things are not that simple. In the mid-1980s senior executives at Morton Thiokol, which made solid-fuel rockets for the NASA space shuttle, were warned by their engineers that a vital component in the booster rockets was problematic and might fail with dire consequences. Morton Thiokol consulted with staff and the majority of staff were in favour of going ahead. They knew that the NASA contract, which was up for renewal, meant jobs for them and they were unwilling to hold up the launch. Only the engineers directly involved in the booster rocket design were strongly opposed. Morton Thiokol withheld this information from NASA. On 28 January 1986, seconds after launching, the booster O-rings on the Challenger rocket failed and all seven astronauts, including a civilian schoolteacher, perished.

The key to procedural justice is flexibility. Different approaches to decision making are appropriate in different circumstances. In this chapter we will see that there are really only four fundamental approaches. Each has its advantages and its drawbacks.

Effective decision making means choosing the best approach to the decision at hand. The trouble is, most people tend to have a preferred approach and stick to it, whatever the situation. If you're lucky, you'll find yourself in a niche where you're only faced with decisions which suit your decision-making style. But maybe you get promotion to a different role where you're faced with a whole different kind of decisions. Your old approach may not work any more. What happens when we use the wrong kind of approach to decisions?

First, the people who are affected by the decisions lose trust in the decision maker. And sometimes a comparatively minor decision can have far-reaching consequences. A moment's inattention to the decision-making process can lead to a lifetime's regret, as Gerald Ratner discovered to his cost. In 1991, 42-year-old Ratner was an extremely successful businessman – so much so that he had been invited to address the British Institute of Directors on the success of the jewellery chain which bore his name. However, he was scheduled to speak in that difficult after-lunch slot when the participants were relaxing after food and wine. He thought a dose of honesty would liven up the proceedings, and so he decided to come clean about what he thought of his company's products. He described them as 'absolute crap'. He elaborated his theme by comparing the product range in durability and price with those of a prawn sandwich. With hindsight it is easy to see that Ratner made the wrong decision. The comments were quickly picked up by the press and the company share price fell from 150p to 15p. Within months Ratner was out of a job and the new owners renamed the chain to try to escape from the 'crap' epithet.

Losing trust

Although a bad decision can harm trust, that is not the end of the story. Human beings find it difficult to admit mistakes and tend to make further decisions to try to justify their initial error. The worse a decision is from the point of view of procedural justice, the less trust there will be. When people are deprived of both distributive and procedural justice, they often seek a third kind – retributive justice. This can take the form of dramatic industrial sabotage, or it can be an everyday occurrence like stealing office supplies. It certainly does nothing for trust.

Retributive justice

If bolstering a poor decision destroys trust, a frank admission that you have made a mistake can do enormous good in rebuilding it. The summer of 1995 was long, hot

Admitting your mistake

and dry in the UK, and Yorkshire Water found itself running out of supplies to the extent that the public were warned to prepare for rota cuts and supplies from standpipes in the streets. An off-the-cuff comment by the then chief executive to the effect that he had not had a bath in the region for months (he frequently visited his mother in Middlesbrough, and took his baths there where supplies were more plentiful) was misinterpreted by the media as advice to the public to stop taking baths. It was a public relations disaster. Despite some remarkable logistic feats of tankering water into the region, Yorkshire Water was soundly criticized at a subsequent public inquiry. When new chief executive Kevin Bond took over in 1996, almost his first action was to speak individually to key regional press and media journalists to say that Yorkshire Water had let its customers down and he wanted to apologize. He then went on to explain how the company was investing some £170 million to ensure that it would be able to cope next time it encountered a similarly dry summer. His willingness to accept responsibility has done much to help the slow process of rebuilding trust.

Is an ability to make good decisions an innate characteristic – something you either have or you don't? How else can we explain that some people seem to be able to reach brilliant decisions quite intuitively while the rest of us are still dithering on the horns of a dilemma? But in the world of organizations and business, the ability to make wonderful decisions on your own isn't necessarily a desirable trait. What is much more valuable is the ability to know the most appropriate way of approaching a decision, and in particular the extent to which you should involve other people.

APPROACHES TO DECISION MAKING

When you are faced with a tricky decision, is your instinct to make your own mind up or to pick other people's brains for ideas? Do you prefer to reach a decision in a logical way, or more intuitively? These questions are important

	Intuitive	Logical
Make up your own mind	Decide and sell	Negotiate
Involve others	Blank sheet consultation	Propose and consult

Figure 2   Approaches to decision making

because they determine your decision-making style.

Figure 2 shows the four main approaches to making a decision. The first is decide and sell – you take the decision by yourself and persuade people that it is the right one afterwards. The second approach is negotiate. You know what you want, but you recognize that a certain amount of bargaining is required to reach a decision which is acceptable to the other parties involved. The third approach is propose and consult – you put forward a proposal and ask other people to comment on your ideas and suggest those of their own. Finally, there is blank sheet consultation – you outline the broad parameters of the decision which must be taken, and ask other people for ideas.

No one approach is right all of the time. The very best decision makers show tremendous flexibility in choosing the right approach for a given set of circumstances – they are good at deciding how to decide. Unfortunately, such people are rare. It is more common to take a particular approach either because it is the only style you personally feel comfortable with, or because the organizational culture demands that this is the way decisions are always handled. Let's look at each of the approaches and consider their merits and drawbacks.

DECIDE AND SELL

If the biggest criticism of your company is 'the higher-ups never ask us for our opinion', then your bosses probably favour a decide and sell approach to decision making. In some companies, not much effort is put into selling the decision, and the style is more like decide and tell. However, times have changed since Stanley Milgram conducted his famous experiments in the 1950s when ordinary people complied with instructions to (so they thought) give other people painful electric shocks simply because someone in authority told them to do so. These days, even in the most autocratic and hierarchical organizations, a certain amount of selling decisions is needed.

As a decision-making approach, decide and sell still has a pretty bad image, for justifiable reasons. If you don't involve people who will be affected by a decision until the point where you are trying to sell it to them, not only will you run the risk of having missed some important pieces of information, but you will find it difficult to get their commitment to implementing whatever the decision is.

However, there are some situations where decide and sell *is* the best way to make a decision. If the decision hinges on some basic issues on which you are not prepared to budge, then decide and sell makes a lot of sense. Core values are an example of a basic issue on which you should not compromise.

In 1982, executives at Johnson & Johnson received the shocking news that several poisonings had occurred in the Chicago area, apparently after taking the company's best-selling pain reliever, Tylenol. It quickly became clear that, after the tablets had left the plant, someone had been lacing them with cyanide. A lively debate immediately started within J&J as to the best way to handle the crisis. The debate was quickly cut short by chairman Jim Burke who immediately ordered the recall of all Tylenol products. For him it was a question of core values – Johnson & Johnson's credo, its statement of business beliefs, begins with responsibility to those who use its products – only at the very end, after affirming commitment to employees and the wider community, does it mention commitment to shareholders and profit. Although Tylenol was worth $100 million a year to the company, the only way in which the company could live up to its credo was to recall all Tylenol products.

It is also appropriate to use decide and sell if you have knowledge or expertise about a problem which no one else possesses. If you are responsible for purchasing a new computer system for your company, then it doesn't make much sense to ask staff to weigh up the technical merits of one system against another if they really don't have the knowledge necessary to make an informed judgement. The pitfall here is that few decisions are best made on technical grounds alone. In this example extensive consultation would have helped determine what your colleagues in the company wanted from their new computer system.

Finally, decide and sell is the best, indeed sometimes the only available, method when time is very short. On 5 August 1949 fifteen trained firefighters parachuted into Mann Gulch to attempt to fight a forest fire raging through the mountains of Montana. The firefighters got into more and more disarray until they found themselves completely surrounded by fire on all sides. At this point, team leader Wagner Dodge gave them an apparently bizarre instruction – to set fire to the ground on which they were standing. This area would then not be able to burn any further. Time was very short, Dodge was pretty sure that only he knew how to save their lives, and he was not prepared to compromise in any way. He did set fire to the spot where they were standing and then lay down in the ashes of his escape fire. He survived. The rest of the team attempted to make a run for it, and all but two lost their lives.

As well as showing that lengthy consultation is not always the way to find the best answer, this example demonstrates the weakness of decide and sell as an approach – it will work only if you have either sufficient authority or trust to make the decision stick. In business, most rushed decisions occur because poor planning has left them to the last minute. It is almost as if an unconscious process operates in the minds of some decision makers – 'If I keep putting off this decision until the last minute then I will have a perfect excuse for deciding myself rather than consulting others because time is so short.' This kind of approach will destroy trust and make implementation difficult.

NEGOTIATE

If you know what you want, but don't have the authority or the influence to persuade others to agree, then you need to negotiate. Is it possible to get the outcome you want and maintain some kind of relationship with the people concerned? Some negotiators are not bothered about relationships – they just want to get their own way. They will use any technique they can lay their hands on to lie, trick or bamboozle you into agreeing to do things their way. Trickery and deceit may get them a result once, but you will never trust them again. Some negotiators go to the other extreme – they are so concerned to maintain the relationship that they give in completely to the other side's demands. This too is self-defeating in the long term. People who give in 'for the sake of a quiet life' may continue to experience an underlying resentment. They too rarely engender the respect or trust of their negotiating partners.

COMPROMISE

That is why so much traditional negotiation is built on compromise. I have £5000 to spend on a secondhand car and you want £6000 for the one you are selling. We agree a compromise of £5500, provided that you throw in a set of tools and I pay you in cash.

Compromise isn't a bad place to be. Each side gets a bit of what it wants, and trust is at least not harmed. But there is another alternative, which is to go for a win/win outcome – a situation where both parties get what they want and trust is enhanced.

The key to win/win outcomes is creativity. Many businesses find themselves locking horns with governments over environmental regulations. Governments want tough environmental regulations to protect both local communities and the planet as a whole. Businesses don't want them because the costs of complying with regulations reduce competitiveness. PR firms and even the courts become involved in what can be an expensive and time-consuming wrangle for both sides. Eventually some kind of compromise is reached – the regulations are not quite as tough as originally proposed, or a longer time is allowed to phase them in. Often, neither side is really satisfied. Businesses face additional costs, even though not quite as much as they had feared – governments slow down the degradation of the environment, but not as effectively as they had hoped.

But a few organizations have taken a different approach. Rather than seeing environmental regulation as a threat, they see it as an opportunity. After all, pollution is just another form of waste, and every company knows that there is profit to be found in eliminating waste. Companies which take a win/win approach look for ways of complying with the regulations *and* reducing costs. For example, most US distillers of coal tar opposed 1991 regulations requiring substantial reductions in benzene emissions. At the time, the only solution was to cover the tar storage tanks with costly gas blankets. But Pittsburgh-based Aristech Chemical Corporation looked for a win/win solution: it developed a way of removing benzene right at the start of the distilling process. This new approach actually saved the company $3.3 million.

The kind of creativity which leads to win/win solutions doesn't have to rely on technology. Sometimes it's just a question of identifying what the other party's interests really are, rather than the positions they are taking for the purposes of negotiation. You'll recall that Leyland Trucks used to have a problem over kettles in the assembly area. Management took the position that the kettles should not be there, workers the position that they should. But the

WIN/WIN OUTCOMES

real issue was not particularly about kettles – it was about the workers' desire to be treated like adults who could help themselves to a hot drink whenever they wanted. Once management realized that this was what mattered, it was easy to come up with the 'creative' solution of providing fixed but accessible hot water boilers.

COPING WITH TOUGH TACTICS

Will your negotiating opponents be dishonest at times? Probably. Negotiation is one area of business where deceit is often tolerated, if not actually encouraged. But if you want to develop a long-term relationship of trust with the other person as well as getting your outcome, this is a dangerous route to follow. Instead, use honesty to your advantage.

The master of using honesty to win difficult negotiations is US lawyer Gerry Spence. He has never lost a criminal case. He even successfully defended Imelda Marcos in the face of universal condemnation from every corner of the media. His view is that if you really tell the truth, not just the facts of the case but the truth about the power you do and don't have in defending it, then you will win the argument every time – and build trust with your erstwhile opponents.

Early in my career as a consultant I tendered for a review of a company's performance-related pay (PRP) scheme. This was an important and high-profile piece of work. In fact the company, which had had performance-related pay for a number of years, wasn't sure whether it wanted to improve the scheme or ditch it altogether. With such a sensitive topic, the company certainly wanted consultants who knew what they were doing, and it had invited a number of well-known firms to bid for the work. I was pleased to be invited to an interview to discuss my proposal. The first question I was asked was: 'What experience do you have of developing or reviewing performance-related pay schemes?' It seems to me that many consultants pretend that they are good at everything – should I conform to the rules of this game and pretend that I had more experience than I actually had? Or should I tell the truth and admit that I had virtually none? What I said was this: 'I don't have any experience of developing or reviewing performance-related pay schemes. But almost by definition, a consultant who does will be an enthusiast for them. It seems to me that you need a consultant who can bring an open mind to the question of whether you need PRP or not. Let me tell you the experience I have which is relevant to this task.' I won the contract.

PROPOSE AND CONSULT

If you don't make the decision yourself then you have to involve other people, and a good way to do this is to propose and consult. If you use this approach skilfully, the benefits are threefold – you get a better decision, more commitment and more trust. As ever, there are pitfalls you must sidestep if these potential benefits are not to be lost.

There are two sets of people you might want to consult with: people who have expertise on the matter at hand, and people who will be affected by the outcome of the decision. In some cases these two sets of people are quite distinct. If you want to decide on a new computer system, you might want to consult with computer experts outside your company on technical aspects of the decision, and with staff who as users will be affected by it. In other cases, the two sets might overlap or even be the same group of people. In company restructurings, staff may be both the experts and the people affected by the change.

There are two principal dangers to be avoided when consulting with experts. The first is to spend too long on the process of consulting and gathering information – analysis paralysis. In the novel *The Dice Man*, the eponymous hero becomes rich and famous by making all of his decisions by throwing dice. While I'm not advocating instant decision making for everything – the Dice Man is a fictional creation – there is a lot to be said for making decisions sooner rather than later.

**CONSULTING THE
EXPERTS**

Too much time

Certainly the trend in strategic planning has moved in this direction. Once upon a time every business worth its salt had a big strategic planning department which extensively and intricately analysed data in order to prepare the right strategy for the company. The trouble is, by the time this had all been done, the strategic plan was already out of date and irrelevant. It's arguable that the world of work is so complex, and changing so rapidly, that searching for the right strategy is misguided. It's a bit like asking if Shakespeare wrote the 'right' *Hamlet*, or Beethoven the 'right' ninth symphony. If strategy is essentially a creative process rather than a scientific one, then you don't look for the 'right' strategy, but one which is elegant and effective. Like the process of creating a play or a piece of music, this approach to strategy is inherently more messy and experimental. Try a lot of things, see what works and quickly ditch the ones which don't.

Too much faith

The second danger when consulting the experts is to put too much faith in their suggestions. No one is as close to your specific decision as you are, although the experts may have masses more experience of very similar decisions. The more complex a decision, the less a standard solution is likely to work. It's a little like someone who goes to an optician to complain about her eyesight. The optician takes off his own glasses and says, 'You should use this prescription – it's served me well for years.' An expert who provides you with advice is a supplier of information and, as we have already seen, the most effective relationships with suppliers are based on trust, and this takes time to develop. Trust is especially needed when the provider of expertise has a vested interest in the outcome of your decision. Giving advice which goes against the short-term business interests of the giver is a good indication that this is a person you can trust.

CONSULTING THE PEOPLE AFFECTED

Consulting with the people who will be affected by the decision is no less problematic, especially if trust is low: provide a detailed proposal and they will say that your mind is already made up; provide only a sketchy idea and they will say that you have given them nothing which is worth responding to. Whatever the level of trust at the start of the consultation process, you need to make three things very clear if you want to raise it:

1. What has already been decided and what is open to change.

2. What consultation means – you are asking for their ideas and you will consider them very carefully, but at the end of the day *you* will decide. Since different people are likely to respond differently to your proposal, at least some of those consulted will be disappointed by the final decision.

3. The mechanics of the consultation process – where to get more information, how to respond, by when and so on.

In many circumstances, a fourth point is also relevant – you may need to educate people to be able to respond productively to your proposal. As a way of building trust and commitment, many organizations share their draft business plans with the workforce and ask for comments. They are often disappointed with the response. But the nature and language of most business plans make them incomprehensible to a normal person doing a normal job, and if organizations really want to know what their employees think about their business plan then they need to educate them first.

BLANK SHEET CONSULTATION

If consultation is such a good thing, why not go the whole hog and use blank sheet consultation? There are two varieties of blank sheet consultation. If you intend to consult with a large number of people then you can seek their views on the basis of a consultation paper or a series of meetings.

If smaller numbers are involved – typically 12 or less – then you have the option to delegate the decision-making authority to them, put them in a room together for a while and see what they come up with. There's certainly a great deal of research evidence which suggests that groups can come up with better solutions to problems than individuals can. Part of the reason for this is that groups get to generate more outlandish and creative ideas. However, there is a downside to this. The group might actually agree to a decision which is highly unsuitable, and which no individual would personally sanction. Psychologist Irving Janis calls this groupthink – when individuals feel that the pressure to conform to the views of their peers outweighs individual judgements which they might otherwise have made about the situation.

Nevertheless, handing over decision-making authority in a blank sheet consultation has a great deal to be said for it. As well as getting more commitment to the final decisions, you are more likely to get interesting and creative ideas. If you take this approach, then the issue of education and training, sometimes a help in propose and consult decisions, becomes vital for blank sheet consultation decisions. Training people in the decision-making process will ensure that time spent building trust up front pays huge dividends in the long term.

HOW TO MAKE EFFECTIVE DECISIONS

CHOOSE THE BEST APPROACH

Your credibility

When you are faced with a particular decision, how do you choose between decide and sell, negotiate, propose and consult and blank sheet consultation? There are four factors to take into account.

If you took this decision, would other people agree to it? If the answer to this question is yes, then decide and sell is an option, as are the two forms of consultation. If the answer is no, you will need to use some form of negotiation, even if only for part of the decision-making process.

If you want other people to be committed to a decision, you are more likely to get it if you use some form of consultation – either propose and consult or blank sheet. More likely, but not guaranteed. The level of commitment depends not only on the method you choose, but on the skill with which you carry it out.

Two organizations decide to introduce a performance appraisal system, and both know that commitment to the new system is going to be crucial to its success. Both decide to take what amounts to a blank sheet consultation approach. Organization X organizes a series of short sessions for all its staff, at which managers explain what performance appraisal is all about and then ask the staff to put forward their views on the key features of such a system. Most staff come up with words like 'fair', 'simple to understand' and 'practical'. The managers of organization X then go away and design a scheme which meets these criteria. It is implemented with a great deal of success. Organization Y sets up a working group, which organizes a similar set of meetings with all staff. These meetings take longer, because they are used to try to draft an actual performance appraisal system. The result of attempting to include everyone's comments is a lengthy and not very inspiring system. No one likes it and it never really gets off the ground.

If you are sure that you have all the information you need to make the decision, then decide and sell is an option. But you need to be sure that you really do have all the information. This is difficult because you don't know what you don't know. If you have enough information to decide the major parameters of a decision, but you need more detail about how it will work in practice, then propose and consult is best. If you need information about fundamental principles before you can make a decision, or if you really need some creative and innovative ideas, then blank sheet consultation is the way to go.

In terms of making a decision, decide and sell is quick, while the other methods can be time consuming. But when

The commitment you need from those affected

The information you need from others

Time

it comes to implementing a decision, the tables are turned: the process of selling the decision can take a very long time indeed, while the consensus which the other methods build can lead to swift implementation.

Westerners who negotiate with Japanese businesspeople can find it frustrating that their Japanese counterparts seem to take so long to make up their minds. Typically Western negotiators arrive with full authority to act on behalf of their companies, while the Japanese negotiators seem to have to consult with a whole bunch of their people before they can respond to anything. But once an agreement is reached, the Japanese can implement it immediately, while Western businesspeople may have a hard task ahead of them selling the deal to their colleagues.

Former ICI chairman John Harvey-Jones reflected on a time when his company was building a new chemical plant, identical to one which was being planned by a Japanese company. Both projects were given the green light at the same time. The British project team quickly made all the key decisions about the plant specification and began to build it:

> After four months we were already breaking ground and priding ourselves in being well ahead of the Far East competition, who were still endlessly debating items of design and equipment. Imagine our chagrin when not only did they complete their plant seven months before us, but it worked first go while ours suffered the usual teething troubles and only achieved its flowsheet [full capacity] some three months after start up.

Combining the approaches

Complex decisions may involve a combination of the methods above. Each year, AES involves all of its staff in the strategic planning process. It begins with each plant having an open-ended one-day planning meeting. This is essentially blank sheet consultation – AES staff say whatever they think should happen to their plant and to the business as a whole. Summaries of each meeting are prepared by a small strategic planning group. These summaries are discussed at a three-day strategic planning retreat, attended by senior managers, plant representatives and anyone else who has a contribution to make. Through negotiation, a draft strategic plan is agreed. This document is circulated to all staff for any further comments – propose and consult – before the plan is implemented by the AES operating committee. This committee, which meets every two months to implement and refine the plan in response to changing conditions, will decide and sell any changes.

Once you have gathered the information you need to analyse it. Three techniques are useful here.

ANALYSE THE INFORMATION

Pros and cons. Simply weigh up the relative merits of the various courses of action open to you. If necessary, score them against appropriate criteria.

For example, you are purchasing a new piece of equipment for your factory and three suppliers have quoted you for their machine. Your criteria are purchase cost, running costs, productivity and maintenance requirements. You should score each supplier's offering against these four criteria.

'What if' analysis, also known as scenario planning. What would be the consequences of pursuing one option rather than another?

Risk and reward. In most cases the higher the reward, the higher the risk – but not always. A careful analysis of risk v reward can help you reach the right decision.

In 1952 four-fifths of Boeing's sales came from one customer – the US Air Force. The company had no presence in the commercial market and all of its attempts to enter it had failed. Nevertheless, it decided to make an enormous investment in developing a commercial jet airliner – for which there was at that time no market demand. If the gamble had failed, then Boeing probably would have folded. But it didn't – the 707 brought the commercial world into the jet age.

CONSULTATION IS NOT NEGOTIATION

Just because you have consulted with people doesn't mean that you are obliged to go with the majority vote. It's your decision, not theirs. Consultation is not negotiation. Sometimes a detailed analysis of all the available information will indicate that you must take a decision against the express wishes of the people you have consulted with.

IMPLEMENT THE DECISION

When decisions are in the offing, it is by definition a time of uncertainty. Until the decision is made, no one knows for sure just what will happen. Uncertainty creates stress. If people aren't told what's going on they'll make it up – and what they imagine will almost certainly be far worse than the reality. You need to communicate at all stages of the decision-making process. At the outset, you need to tell people what the process will be. During the decision-making process you need to let people know how things are progressing, especially if there have been any changes from what you originally told them. You also need to remind them how they contribute to the process. Once the decision is made you need to communicate what the decision is and how it will be implemented.

Many organizations conduct a decision-making process which is faultless from the trust perspective and then throw it all away when they implement it. There are two ways of implementing a decision – the big bang approach, where everything happens at once; and phasing in, where the decision is implemented more gradually over a period of time.

The big bang approach has the merit of speed, and some circumstances can justify it. More often, some kind of phasing in is more appropriate. The decision can be phased in everywhere over time, or it might be fully implemented first in one location then in another, in a process usually known as piloting. Piloting has great advantages – it reduces the risk of a major disaster because you can learn from your mistakes as you go along. It also reduces the fear of the unknown, which is a big factor in resistance to organizational change.

MANAGEMENT STRUCTURE

One way of thinking about your company's management structure is to consider it as a decision-making process set in stone. The more hierarchical and rigid the management structure, the more inflexible and ineffective the decision-making process. And some companies can be very inflexible.

When Mike Walsh took over as CEO of Union Pacific Railroad (UPRR) in 1986, his first priority was to meet as many front-line railroaders as he could, face to face. One such meeting was arranged at the Jenks Shop, a big locomotive repair depot in Arkansas, and Walsh sent a memo asking everybody to prepare some questions for his visit. Did this memo go straight on to the workshop noticeboard? No – the workshop manager decided that he didn't have the authority to act on it, so he sent it to his general manager in Texas. The general manager returned it saying that he didn't have the authority to decide either, but that the mechanical department in Omaha did. The head of the mechanical department duly made the decision that it was OK for Mike Walsh's memo to appear on the noticeboard at the Jenks repair depot.

If this story seems unbelievable, it was only too typical of how UPRR operated at that time. Matters needing to be decided were routinely passed up and down the company before anyone actually made the decision. Unsurprisingly, the railroad was losing money hand over fist.

One of the first things Walsh did was to reduce the hierarchy and put as much responsibility for decision making at the local level as possible. When he arrived there were 10 levels of management between a railroader and the operations vice president. After Walsh's reorganization there were just five.

There are many benefits to delayering an organization's management. It saves a lot of money, it speeds up communication and it forces managers to make people truly accountable. Most importantly, it enables organizations to take a much more flexible approach to decision making.

Act with Integrity *8*

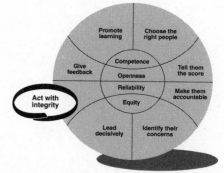

Every good relationship – whether between a husband and wife, between friends, or between employer and employee – is built on a foundation of trust. Trust allays our fears of betrayal by people we depend on, whether at home or work.

Charles Fombrun

*I*F people are going to be able to rely on you, then they need to be confident that you will act with integrity. At its most basic, this means keeping your promises – doing what you say you will do. This practice is by no means as common as it could be; one recent survey at British Telecom found that only one in five employees trusted their managers to do what they said they would do. But reliability is more than this – it means acting in a consistent way that people can depend on.

How do you maintain that fine balance between consistency and inflexibility? By ensuring that your behaviour is consistent with your values. Even this is not sufficient for people to rate you as totally dependable: you must also act to the highest ethical standards. As we shall see later in this chapter, in a world where you are judged against many different standards, this is the hardest skill of all.

KEEP YOUR PROMISES

Broken promises don't just reduce levels of trust – they annihilate it. Listen to this bus driver talking about trust.

> Of course we don't trust the management – why should we? In the past the buses have always been fuelled up and safety checked for us before we take them out on a shift – now we've been told that we have to do this ourselves. Our union called a meeting with one of the managers about this and, to give him his due, he did listen to us. 'I'll get back to you next Wednesday,' he said. Of course we never heard from him again and that was three weeks ago. We're still late setting out on every run because we have to fuel and check ourselves – it's the customers who suffer. We've also been told that we will be getting another pay cut. This is definitely the last pay cut, the management have told us, just like they told us the last two pay cuts were definitely the last. It's no wonder that none of the drivers trust management.

If breaking promises is a quick way to destroy trust, keeping them is a very speedy way to establish it. You meet a business acquaintance and during the course of your conversation you discover that you have a report or article which will be of interest to her. You promise to hunt it out and send it. The next day, it appears on her desk. With this simple action you have already strengthened your reputation for being trustworthy. Unless she knows you well, the chances are that your business acquaintance will also be a little surprised. Why? Because keeping promises, crucial though it is to trust, often doesn't happen much in the workplace.

When your work colleagues say they will do something by such and such a time, how often do they stick to that promise? 100 per cent of the time? Unlikely. 75 per cent? 50 per cent? In places where promises count for little, meetings start late, decisions take months, and staff spend much of their time chasing things that someone else should have done.

One of the consequences of competition in business, and especially of global competition, is that organizations are under ever-increasing expectations to produce more and more from less and less. This is great for consumers, but not so good for employees. You have to work harder or you have to work smarter – either way more people are going to be asking you to do more for them. In the face of these expectations it is easy to cave in and say 'I'll do my best'. You overcommit yourself. When there just aren't enough hours in the day to honour all your commitments, you have to let some go by the wayside. Your reputation for being reliable and trustworthy begins to seep away.

You needn't feel too ashamed of this – organizations do this too. As the Union Pacific Railroad's vice president for customer service, Bill Hillebrandt, commented:

> We didn't know how to say 'no'. A customer would ask for something, we would say 'sure'. But we didn't have the faintest idea of whether or not we could do the job.

The trouble is that once an organization gets a reputation for being unreliable, its customers tend to go elsewhere. That's why the railroads lost so much business in the early 1980s to the road haulage companies – the truckers weren't cheaper and they weren't always faster either, but they were certainly a lot more reliable. UPRR only began to compete again once it had built a reputation for reliability. And you need to do the same.

Stress

Breaking promises creates stress. Let's say you promise to send a report to a colleague by the end of the week. Friday comes and goes and on Monday morning your colleague immediately has a dilemma – should she chase you for the report or just hope that it will turn up? Depending on the relationship between you and your colleague, other things might start to happen too. She might think you consider her unimportant because you haven't bothered to get her the report. Perhaps you don't really trust her with the information the report contains.

If all this sounds implausible, haven't you ever been in a situation when you have imagined all sorts of sinister reasons why someone has failed to do something for you, when in reality they've simply forgotten? Or perhaps they've 'forgotten' for a reason.... You can end all these shenanigans and the stress that goes with them simply by keeping your promises.

KNOW YOUR CAPABILITIES

In Chapter 5 we saw how important it was to assess the capabilities of another person before entrusting them with responsibility. The same applies to you. Before agreeing to take on a task you need to assess yourself. Can you deliver? In some cases you may well have the skills to do the task, but not have the time to do it bearing in mind all the other things you have to do.

Keep a time log

Do you know how much you can achieve in a day? Or do you tend to overcommit? If so, you need to get a more accurate picture of how you spend your time. Keep a time log – an exact record of how you spend each 15 minutes in the day from the moment you arrive at work until the moment you leave. At the end of each day, review how you've spent your time and what you have achieved. After a week you will have a much better idea of what you are capable of achieving in a given amount of time.

A colleague urgently needs some information which only you can provide, but you're up to your eyes in doing something for an important client. You know in your heart that what you should say is: 'I can't do this until the end of the week.' But if you do say this your colleague will be irritated, so you say instead: 'I'll try to get it done by the end of the day', knowing that this is impossible.

Make specific promises

Get into the habit of making very clear, specific promises. Whenever you hear yourself saying something

like: 'I'll do my best to have it done this week', pull
yourself up and say instead: 'I'll do it by next Thursday' or
whatever it is realistic to promise. A specific promise is
better for the other person – they know more precisely
when you will deliver – and it is better for you because it
gives you more incentive to do the task on time. If you
really are unable to achieve a task within the timescale
required, you should say no.

What if you have the time to do the task, but you are
not sure about whether you have the skills to achieve it?
You need to have a good knowledge of your own skills and
a commitment to developing them. We'll see how you can
do this in the next two chapters.

All work falls into one of four categories:

KNOW YOUR PRIORITIES

Talking to a customer about a complaint is important and
urgent.

1 Important and urgent

Training and staff development are important, rarely
urgent – there is usually no problem if they are delayed for
a few days or weeks. Problems occur when the weeks
become months or even years, and something which is
important does not get done.

2 Important but not urgent

Much of the internal bureaucracy of organizational life falls
into this category. Organizations run on power-based
relationships tend to have a lot of this non-value-adding
work.

3 Urgent but not important

Another name for this category is 'timewasters'. There are
the obvious ones, like the people who drop into your
office to complain to you about how busy they are. There
are also more subtle timewasters: junk mail; meetings you
attend because you feel you ought to be there, even when
it is not clear what you put into or get out of them; the
trade journals you skim through 'just in case' there is
anything important, even though there rarely is.

*4 Not urgent and not
important*

Your priorities should be categories 1 and 2 – the important things. In particular, you need to resist the temptation to put off category 2 – important but not urgent – and deal with category 3 – urgent but not important – instead.

ACT FAST WHEN LAPSES OCCUR

Recall Intel's failure with the Pentium chip described in Chapter 6 and contrast this with Johnson & Johnson's handling of the Tylenol case described in the last chapter. High trust organizations realize that a lapse of reliability – real or perceived – is an opportunity to build a bond of trust with their customers, provided that the lapse is dealt with speedily and effectively. In *Credibility*, James Kouzes and Barry Posner offer a six-step plan for dealing with foul-ups:

- Accept personal responsibility for dealing with the shortcoming

- Admit that a mistake has been made

- Apologize for the inconvenience

- Act immediately to do what you can there and then to remedy things

- Make amends by offering some form of recompense

- Attend to the long-term needs of the relationship.

However conscientious you are, you will occasionally find yourself unable to keep a promise. If, like Intel, you simply wait to be found out, your reputation for reliability and trustworthiness will be damaged. But if you respond quickly, like Johnson & Johnson, you can actually enhance your reputation.

Let's say that you promised a colleague a report by the end of the day and you are unable to deliver. Don't wait for her to chase you once the deadline has passed. Act before the deadline is reached. Contact your colleague, accept responsibility, admit you're going to miss the deadline and apologize. Agree a new deadline. Make amends by offering some form of recompense and attend to the relationship over the long term.

The main thing which distinguishes people who consistently keep their promises from those who do not isn't their skills, it's their mindset. People who let others down tend to see themselves as victims of circumstances. You can spot it in the way they talk. Think of people who frequently use phrases like:

DO YOU BELIEVE IT IS POSSIBLE TO HONOUR PROMISES?

- I had to, there was no option.

- He made me feel guilty.

- There's nothing to do but grin and bear it.

Some people have a fundamental belief that there's not much you can do to influence what happens to you. You just have to accept what comes along. If that's your belief, then you are going to find it hard to keep promises, because things will just keep popping up and getting in the way.

Other people see nothing but opportunities. They have an essentially proactive outlook. They feel deeply responsible for their own destiny. They see their role as going out and changing things for the better.

Of course, neither of these extreme views is demonstrably true. It is as difficult to prove that we are entirely driven by events beyond our control as it is to prove that we are entirely in control of everything we do. Beliefs don't have to be provable or even rational.

The question is, which belief is more useful? If you want to be trusted and you want many other things too – like success in business – there's no contest. It's much more useful to believe that we have a lot of influence over what goes on in our lives. If this becomes a self-fulfilling prophecy, so much the better.

If you want to have a proactive attitude to life, there are two beliefs that are very useful to have. The first of these is: 'I can choose how I feel'.

I CAN CHOOSE HOW I FEEL

For some people, this is an incredible statement. Surely you just feel however you feel and that's the end of it? But for others, a fundamental aspect of being responsible for your own life is to choose how to feel in certain circumstances.

Let's say you mess up an important business presentation. Most people would experience some displeasure at this. But some people continue to feel bad about it for hours, days, months and even years afterwards. Others are able to say, 'OK, I fouled up. What can I learn from this and how can I move on?' I'm not saying that you should be able to throw some internal switch and feel any emotion in response to any situation – that would be a very bizarre way to live your life. But I am saying that it is good to be able to choose an appropriate response to external circumstances. If you make a mistake, beating yourself up for months to come is not an appropriate or useful response.

I ALWAYS HAVE OPTIONS

All too often, it's easy to believe that we either have no choice at all, or we have a straight choice between one thing and another. Typically, proactive people believe that they have lots of choices. For them, it's not just A or B: it's C, D, E and F. High trust organizations are very comfortable with this way of thinking. They don't choose between the autocracy of the power-based relationship and the abdication of the hope-based relationship – they find an altogether better way in the shape of trust-based relationships.

In circumstances of high trust, all sorts of new and innovative options become possible. During the filming of *Raiders of the Lost Ark*, director Stephen Spielberg had planned a marvellous fight scene between the whip-wielding Indiana Jones and an Arabian swordsman. He had carefully scripted the scene to be the most extraordinary whip versus sword fight in cinema history. When the time came to shoot the scene on location in Tunisia, actor Harrison Ford was suffering from both heat exhaustion and gastroenteritis and was not up to the physical demands of the proposed scene. It looked like the only option was an expensive delay in the shooting schedule. Then Spielberg, Ford and the rest of the team improvised a scene in which Indiana Jones simply pulls out his gun and shoots the swordsman. This became one of the most memorable moments in the film. Abandoning the original plan was only possible because of the trust which existed between Spielberg and his actors and crew.

As well as creating extra choices, proactive people like to combine apparent alternatives into a new option. Let's not choose A or B – let's find a way to do A *and* B. We've encountered this phenomenon in the guise of win/win outcomes from successful negotiations. High trust organizations like this approach. For example, they don't choose between stability and change – they do both. They adhere to a set of enduring values while committing themselves to learning and change in achieving them.

New options

ALIGN YOUR BEHAVIOUR WITH YOUR VALUES

I once went to collect my car after it had been serviced. There was some delay in finding the car keys and eventually a shamefaced receptionist had to tell me that she was very sorry, but the mechanic had gone off to lunch and mistakenly taken my car keys with him. This in itself was somewhat unsatisfactory from my point of view, but what made it worse was the fact that written in huge letters on the wall of the reception area was a statement of the company's number one priority – customer satisfaction. From a trust-building perspective, failing to live up to your espoused values is probably worse than having no values at all. Incidentally, that's one reason why it is foolhardy to go around proclaiming that people are the company's greatest asset. The moment anyone is laid off, credibility is lost. To her credit, the receptionist who was looking after me did all the right things in terms of accepting, admitting, apologizing and acting to make amends, but a reduction in the cost of having my car serviced didn't really make up for the waste of my time. The damage had been done.

This incident is as nothing compared to what goes on in some companies. Consultants TJ and Sandra Larkin tell the tale of a large manufacturing company undergoing major change. They brought together thousands of employees to witness the unveiling of the company's new slogan – Trust, Teamwork and Tomorrow. As the staff left the presentation they received caps and coffee mugs inscribed with the three Ts. No sooner was the presentation over than employees discovered that the company had secretly hired private investigators to watch employees for drugs and theft. In fact, some of these investigators had been present during the Trust, Teamwork and Tomorrow launch. The Larkins make the point that when organizations go through big changes, it is better to give people the simple facts, rather than dress them up with all kinds of fancy talk.

This isn't to say that values are unimportant – as we have seen, they are fundamental to a high trust organization. But values only mean something when you act consistently with them. The Larkins' take on this is simple: if you break the rule that values are best communicated through actions, not words, employees will punish you. This can lead to an apparent paradox. Some of the organizations which are most value driven, like First Direct and Northern Foods, are not that keen to talk, publicly at least, about what those values are; they prefer to be judged by their actions. The opposite can also be the case.

What goes for organizations goes for all of the people in them. How do you know whether you are acting consistently with your values? Recall for a moment an occasion when you were away from home on business for a while, and when you got back you were really glad to see someone – and you told them so. How did that feel? Now think of a time when someone asked you to do something and you agreed to do it, even though you really didn't want to. How did that feel? It's unlikely that you experienced the same feelings in both circumstances. In the first situation, you were probably acting consistently with your values when you told the person that you were glad to be back. In the second situation you were probably acting inconsistently. Most of us experience some negative feelings when our actions are at odds with our values.

These are comparatively trivial examples, but it is well worth being aware of these different kinds of feelings so that you know when you are acting inconsistently. Sometimes, however, you know that there is a potential conflict of values and action, but you don't know what to do. Consider these scenarios:

You promise one of your team that you will use the only free hour in your diary this week to coach him through a particularly difficult customer service issue. Later that day your boss demands that you spend that hour with her instead. What do you do?

You've got stuck halfway through drafting an important report, so you decide to take it home with you and work on it that evening. When you get home you discover that your teenage son needs you to spend time with him instead. Whose needs get met?

Sometimes it seems that the only way to honour a commitment to one person is to let down another. But if you are clear about your personal values, then the choice is easier. If know that you value supporting your staff above placating your boss, then the choice is made. Even if your boss doesn't agree, the chances are that she'll respect you for your principles. And you'll feel good about yourself, knowing that you've made a decision based on principle, not expediency. If you know that spending time with your family is important to you, then you won't allow yourself to take work home at the last minute like this. On the other hand, if you are clear that work must take more priority at the moment, and have communicated this to your family, then your son will understand on this occasion.

Principle, not expediency

Don't get me wrong – handling such dilemmas doesn't suddenly become easy just because you know what your values are. But it is certainly a great deal easier than handling them when you don't know what you believe in.

What really matters?

How do you decide what values and beliefs really matter to you? One way is to think what you would like to read in your own obituary. When your time is finally up – as one day it surely will be – what do you want to be remembered for?

One person who appreciated this way of thinking was Alfred Nobel. By 1888 Alfred and his brother Ludwig had made a fortune from oil and munitions. When Ludwig died, some of the newspapers at the time confused the two and printed obituaries of Alfred instead. He was so distressed to read of himself as the dynamite king who had made a fortune by finding new ways to maim and kill others that he rewrote his will, leaving his money for the establishment of the Nobel prizes.

ACT TO THE HIGHEST ETHICAL STANDARDS

Aligning your behaviour to your values is important, but not just any old values will do. You must act to the highest ethical standards.

The subject of business ethics is a vast and complex one. Let's take an overview of the major issues and see how they are related to trust.

Money

There is near universal agreement that taking money which doesn't belong to you is unethical. Nick Leeson went to prison because he used large amounts of cash which properly belonged to his employer, Barings Bank. Stew Leonard, owner of the Norfolk, Connecticut, dairy firm praised in so many Tom Peters books, was sentenced to four years in prison and fined $947,000 because of his part in an elaborate $17 million tax fraud. When Sears Auto Centers in California and New Jersey were accused of selling customers parts and services they didn't need, most people considered that unethical – including Sears CEO Ed Brennan who published an apology in newspapers across the country.

If taking money which doesn't belong to you is wrong, what about giving it – in the form of bribes? In most Western countries the issue is clear cut. But in many parts of the world, exchanging personal gifts as part of a business transaction has a long pedigree. In Japan, for example, it is quite normal to do so.

Carl Kotchian, president of Lockheed Aircraft Corporation in the 1970s, knew this – he also knew that losing a potential $430 million order to airline Nippon would mean large-scale redundancies back home. To ensure the purchase of 20 TriStar aircraft, Kotchian allowed $3.8 million to be paid to various officials and representatives of the then Japanese prime minister. As he subsequently realized, Kotchian had acted unethically. His actions lost him his job and did Lockheed a great deal of damage from which it has never recovered.

Even in those parts of the world where bribery is commonplace, it is still unethical to give or accept bribes. Attempts have often been made to pressure Brazilian company Semco into giving bribes and unofficial payments to various government inspectors and officials – and it has resisted on every occasion. As Ricardo Semler says:

> This has caused us plenty of trouble, but it's worth it rather than send a signal to our employees that we tolerate dishonesty.

High trust organizations do take a high moral stand on this issue. Motorola, for example, has a code of conduct which states:

> Employees of Motorola will respect the laws, customs and traditions of each country in which they operate, but will, at the same time, engage in no course of action which, even if legal, customary, and accepted in any such country, could be deemed to be in violation of the accepted business ethics of Motorola or the laws of the United States relating to business ethics.

Bribes

What goes hand in hand with this statement is the frequently repeated account of how Motorola's CEO in the 1950s walked away from a $10 million deal with a South American government that would have increased the company's profits by nearly 25 per cent, rather than giving bribes to the officials involved.

Child labour

Many of the handmade carpets sold in Western countries are manufactured in the Indian state of Uttar Pradesh. It is estimated that of the 100,000 young boys working in the carpet-making industry, many are effectively slaves, sleeping on the premises, terrorized by the loom owners, working 15 hours a day in dark, airless and extremely hot mudbrick huts with no real meal breaks and minimal or no wages. If this figure is frightening, according to the International Labour Organization there are at least 250 million child workers worldwide.

Most people would agree that child labour is unethical, but what to do about it is another question. In 1992 there were an estimated 75,000 children under 14 working in the Bangladeshi garment industry, mostly girls. The following year, the US government passed the Child Labor Deterrence Act, which had been introduced by senator Tom Harkin. As a result, an estimated 50,000 of these children lost their jobs. But with no other source of income for them or their families, many were forced to turn to harsher ways of earning a living – stone crushing, street hustling or prostitution.

Complex ethical problems require complex solutions. One of the first Western companies to take its responsibilities in this area seriously was Levi-Strauss. In one case, it worked out an agreement with one of its Bangladeshi suppliers that it would remove under 14-year-olds from its workforce but continue to pay wages while they were at school. They would then be reemployed at the age of 14.

Safety

Another difficult area for corporate ethics is safety. In the 1960s the Ford Motor Company discovered a fault with cars in its Pinto range. If another car crashed into a Pinto, even at relatively modest speeds, the petrol tank would explode, with a high risk of killing the occupants of either car. Rather than withdraw the range, Ford executives engaged in some macabre calculations. They weighed up the likelihood of the Pinto being involved in accidents; the chances of deaths ensuing; the probable claims against the company should these cases come to court. These executives concluded that it was more cost-effective to continue to sell the Pinto as built than to withdraw or modify the range. When the Pinto episode came to the public's attention, the company was judged to be acting unethically, and Ford suffered as a result of its customers' lack of trust.

Many companies now stress that the safety of their customers and employees is a prime concern. The problem is that there is no clear distinction between safe and dangerous – it's just that some things are safer than others. As Ralph Nader pointed out, a motor car is to some degree unsafe at any speed. With safety, as with a number of ethical issues – including environmental impact – acting with integrity means working not to absolute standards, but to the highest standards of the time. Producing cars without toughened windscreens, for example, was considered ethical in the 1950s but would not be now.

In the same week that its then chief executive Cedric Brown was awarded a 75 per cent pay rise to £475,000, privatized utility British Gas told staff in its high street showrooms that they would be either laid off or subject to a pay freeze. One survey found that boardroom salaries at the newly privatized utilities had risen sixfold since 1986, to an average of £150,000, while the pay of the average worker had less than doubled, to around £18,000. In the US, the compensation package for the average CEO is 225 times greater than the pay of the average employee in the company. Is this ethical or not?

Pay

Here we are in very murky waters indeed. On the one hand no one is suggesting that everyone should be paid the same; on the other hand there is widespread unease, to say the least, about whether some people deserve the

Resolving ethical dilemmas

levels of remuneration they receive. What is certain is that such extremes are rarely to be found in high trust organizations. CEOs and senior managers do earn more than other employees – but in high trust organizations the other employees do pretty well too, often thanks to generous profit-sharing or stock ownership plans.

Acting to the highest ethical standards is not easy. In some cases, there is general agreement on what is right and wrong. In others, you need to take into account the prevailing standards of the country or of the time. Even where a company is acting unethically – for example in using suppliers which have dubious employment practices – the right action may not always be obvious.

In resolving any ethical dilemma, there is one very important question to ask: **what if everyone concerned found out about this?** As communication technology becomes more effective and more widespread, the chances are that these days everyone will find out about it – whatever it is. And when people do find out, if they judge your behaviour to be unethical, trust will disappear. Regaining this trust – particularly regaining the trust of your customers – will be hard to do.

Give Feedback 9

Frankness is not an admired characteristic amongst British people, and in some cases is actually considered to be slightly uncouth. Truthfulness and openness are particularly difficult aims to have in a British organization where so much of our education and background has been devoted to concealing our feelings and to suffer heroically without protest.

John Harvey-Jones

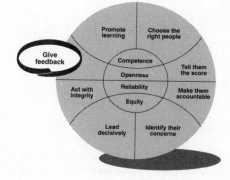

*I*F you want to be able to trust others, you have to be open with them. In Chapter 4 we saw how telling people the score about business objectives and values was an essential part of being open in a high trust organization. But if people are going to be able to trust you, they need more than the confidence that you will share business information with them. They need to have the confidence that you will be equally open when it comes to individual feedback.

As psychologist William James noted:

The deepest principle in human nature is the craving to be appreciated.

People need to know first that you notice what they do, and second that you are prepared to tell them the truth about their behaviour – good and bad. What kind of organization would it be if no one ever gave anyone else any feedback? Of course, some people would hit on the right things by accident, or by their own good judgement. But a lot of time would be wasted, because people would blithely continue doing the wrong things, and no one would ever tell them.

If you think this sounds bad, the situation in many low trust organizations is even worse. People don't get told to their face how they are doing, good or bad – everyone else in the organization is told instead. The phenomenon of gossiping behind people's backs is all too common in the workplace and, needless to say, does nothing to promote trust.

National culture

Giving feedback to another person doesn't always come naturally. As John Harvey-Jones notes, this is partly a question of national culture. Different cultures value straight talking to different degrees. The Dutch and Swedes have a reputation for blunt speaking and delivering the news, whether good or bad. Giving positive feedback comes naturally to many North Americans, although they can sometimes be almost as reticent as their British cousins when it comes to criticism. Japanese people will go to great lengths to avoid anything which can be construed as personal criticism.

Do it the right way

Many people fear that giving feedback will harm a relationship. The opposite is true, provided that the feedback is given in the right way. The way you give someone feedback is usually more critical than the feedback itself. If you don't believe me, try this. Think of a very trivial piece of criticism that you might want to give to a colleague – that his desk is a little untidy, for example. Wait for a time when he is really stressed, and then shout at him – preferably in front of other people – 'You are an untidy person!' Will that harm the relationship? It sure will. In fact, even praise can harm a relationship if it is delivered badly, and comes across as patronizing or manipulative.

By contrast, think of a time when you had to give someone some bad news, or very critical personal feedback. You thought long and hard about when and where you would tell them, and you chose your words carefully. You then went on to tell them in a way which was sensitive and respectful, and your relationship with them was enhanced. Have you had this experience? If you have, then you'll know that the way in which you give feedback is more important than what the actual feedback is. If you haven't had this kind of experience, then you really do need to read the next section!

HOW TO GIVE EFFECTIVE FEEDBACK

Effective feedback has two qualities: the message is delivered in such a way that the person receiving it is able to act on it; and the relationship of trust between the giver and the receiver is maintained or enhanced.

There are a few basic dos and don'ts when it comes to delivering feedback. It's usually best to give someone feedback privately, rather than in front of another person. This is especially true of negative feedback – criticism. The shorter the gap between the feedback and the event which it's about, the better. If you know someone has done something unproductive, don't give them the opportunity to repeat the mistake over and over again – tell them as soon as you reasonably can.

CHOOSE THE RIGHT SETTING

Most importantly, you need to ensure that there is a level of rapport between you and the other person. We've discussed rapport before in terms of matching your physiology to that of the other person, and in terms of using the kind of language which makes sense to them. Tone of voice is a significant factor – the same words can come across very differently depending on how they are spoken. Above all, you need to be sure that the person is really ready to hear what you have to say.

Rapport

Consider this situation: you have just been taken by your new boss to watch him do a presentation to a group of potential customers. The presentation is technically accurate and very slick. But you consider some of the jokes to be of very dubious taste and you also think it patronizing of the customers it was aimed at. He asks you what you thought of his presentation. What do you say? Does he really want quality, accurate feedback, or just a pat on the back from a new acolyte? You would be wise to find out before giving the feedback.

Are they willing to listen?

There's no point in giving feedback unless the person receiving it is going to act on it. They aren't going to act on feedback unless they really want to hear it. Before giving feedback, check that the person is **willing to listen** to you. Sometimes, you just need to ask: 'Would you like some feedback?' Sometimes it's useful to agree a mutual exchange of feedback. This is particularly appropriate if you and a colleague have just undertaken some joint task together. Sometimes, your role as manager effectively gives you authority to give feedback to (and receive it from) your staff. Your company may well have some kind of appraisal system to make this easier – of which more anon. Even so, it's worth checking that the person is willing to listen. Even when someone initiates the discussion by asking you for feedback, still take the trouble to find out how much feedback they really want.

Sometimes it's right to give feedback, even if you are not completely sure that you have the person's permission. The name of George C. Marshall is best known outside the US for his work in aiding the reconstruction of Western Europe after the devastation of the Second World War. What became known as the Marshall Plan was instrumental not only in drastically reducing the levels of poverty and hunger in both victorious and defeated countries, but also in securing long-term political stability. But Marshall also played a large part in winning the war, not only through his actions as an army commander but through his ability to be honest when the situation demanded it. In 1938 Marshall attended his very first briefing with President Franklin D Roosevelt, who laid out an ambitious plan to build 10,000 war planes. After the presentation, Roosevelt asked his listeners if he had made a good case for the programme. Marshall replied sharply, 'I am sorry, Mr President, but I don't agree with you at all.' He then went on to point out that Roosevelt had completely omitted to think about how the planes would be serviced and crewed. Everyone who attended the briefing was shocked by the frankness of the relatively inexperienced Marshall's comments. The Secretary to the Treasury clearly thought Marshall had gone too far and said to him, 'Well, it's been nice knowing you.' In fact, Marshall's intervention had a very positive effect on the President. From then on and throughout the war, Marshall was one of Roosevelt's key advisers. The normally reticent Marshall knew that he had to speak – failure to do so would only store up trouble for later.

Consider these pieces of feedback:

MAKE THE FEEDBACK BEHAVIOURAL

1 You were 10 minutes late for that meeting.

2 You lack time management skills.

3 You have a bad attitude to punctuality.

4 You are a bad timekeeper.

They all address much the same issue, but in different ways. The first statement – you were 10 minutes late for that meeting – is a statement about the person's behaviour. The second alludes to the person's skills, the third says something about their attitude and the fourth makes a judgement about their identity – you are a bad timekeeper. This is not just a question of semantics: people react in very different ways to these different methods of making the point.

In most cases people will not only find the behavioural statement the easiest to listen to, but it's also the one they are most likely to take action on. Apart from anything else, it is by far the easiest to do something about: if you were

10 minutes late for that meeting, you can choose to be on time for the next one. But if you lack time management skills, then that is a harder nut to crack. When I was 12 years old, a music teacher told me that I could not sing. This feedback was not about my behaviour – I was singing too high, or too flat or whatever, but a statement about my skills – he was telling me that I could not sing. It was a useless piece of feedback. I spent the next 15 years of my life miming on any occasion that required me to sing. Feedback at the level of attitude or identity is no better in this respect.

Accuracy

If you are going to give someone useful feedback, then it has to be accurate. When you give behavioural feedback, it's fairly easy to make sure that it is accurate. Provided that you know what time the meeting was scheduled to begin at, and your watch works OK, then the chances are that the feedback 'You were 10 minutes for that meeting' will be accurate.

However, as soon as you start making comments about skills, attitudes or identity, you are on very shaky ground indeed. If someone is late for a meeting, then all you can reliably say is that they were late for the meeting. You really don't know why – maybe they do lack time management skills, maybe they do have a set of attitudes which regulates their punctuality, maybe they do have a personality disorder, but unless you can read their mind you really won't know. So giving feedback at any level other than the behavioural is not only less likely to lead to change, it's less likely to be accurate in any case.

Effective feedback should always be behavioural. It might describe the other person's behaviour, or it might describe the effect of their behaviour on you. For example, it can be useful to say: 'I felt annoyed when you were 10 minutes late for the meeting' or 'I was relieved to see you when you arrived 10 minutes late for the meeting'.

Consider this statement:

'Everyone was annoyed when you arrived 10 minutes late for the meeting.'

Whether this constitutes useful feedback depends on whether it is true or not. If everyone really was annoyed, you know that and you think the other person needs to know, then it is useful feedback. But if you don't really know whether anyone else was annoyed but you just want to raise the emotional temperature a little, then it's not going to be useful.

Begin with behaviour

Once you have given the feedback in behavioural terms, then you can enter into a discussion about it – preferably a discussion which focuses on the future rather than constantly reliving the past. As the person who has received the feedback begins to wonder how they will do things differently next time, the conversation may well turn to issues of skills, attitudes and identity. You may have suggestions for the person to consider. You will have moved on from feedback to problem solving.

GET THE RIGHT BALANCE

Many people tend to think of feedback in terms of criticism, but giving positive feedback – affirmation that the person is doing the right thing – is equally important. Because many people are unused to receiving genuine praise, it is just as important to think carefully about how to deliver it as it is with criticism. As well as reinforcing effective behaviour – and it is surprising how often people do not know that they are doing the right thing – positive feedback is great at building self-esteem.

Self-esteem

You may at times feel like hauling one of your team members in front of you and listing 20 things that she has done to infuriate you today, but if the only effect is to shatter her self-esteem, then your time will have been wasted. Judge the relationship you have with the person – how much feedback can they take from you? Just because you heard your colleague's five-year-old daughter saying 'You're too fat daddy' doesn't mean that it's OK for you to give him the same message. Judge the amount of positive and negative feedback which will be useful to the other person. Even in the closest working relationships, more than three items of criticism at any one time will probably prove too much.

RECEIVING FEEDBACK

If you want people to be open with others, then it is only fair that they are open with you. You should only give feedback if you are able to accept it too. In fact, if you are serious about being trusted, you will want as much feedback as you can get, because it will help you develop your competence.

Receiving feedback requires almost as much skill as giving it. The person you are receiving the feedback from may not be as skilled as you are at giving it. You will have to help them.

- If someone chooses an inappropriate setting for giving you feedback, suggest another one.

- If they give you feedback in terms of your skills, attitudes or identity, ask them what it is they've seen you doing.

- If they overload you with too much feedback – particularly criticism – tell them to stop, or ask them for some positive feedback too.

In some ways, positive feedback – praise – is the hardest to deal with. In many cultures, we are so unused to it that it makes us either embarrassed or suspicious.

We each have our own techniques for avoiding hearing positive feedback. We discount it – we are waiting for the person to say 'but' and give the bad news. We devalue it with comments like: 'It was nothing', 'I was just lucky', 'You'd have done the same'. Or we feel obliged to tell the other person how wonderful they are, in return for the praise they are giving us. We fail to hear feedback properly because we are desperately trying to think up ways of complimenting the other person.

When you receive positive feedback, avoid doing any of these – simply listen carefully and thank the person. If appropriate, ask for more detail: 'You said that was an excellent presentation, thank you, what was it that you particularly liked?'

PERFORMANCE APPRAISAL

In the first part of this chapter we've been considering what you can do to improve the levels of feedback and trust within your area of influence. Although they may be beyond your immediate influence, your organization's systems and structures make a big difference to the levels of trust within it. As far as feedback is concerned, one organizational system is paramount: performance appraisal.

Let's look at the different approaches to performance appraisal, and their effect on trust.

There is a cartoon of four Neolithic cave dwellers. Two of them are carving rocks into perfectly round wheel shapes. The third is carving a strange triangular shape. The fourth figure does not carve, but is watching the other three and hitting the triangle carver on the head with a large club. The cartoon is labelled 'early management techniques'.

FIRST-GENERATION APPRAISAL

Throughout most of the history of work organizations this is about as sophisticated as management techniques got. You learned what to do, usually by watching others, and if you got it wrong somebody gave you a sharp and immediate rebuke. The idea of saving up feedback for some meeting which happened only once a year would have been regarded as ridiculous.

Nevertheless, the first formal appraisal systems were introduced in the early 1950s. These first-generation appraisal systems had little do with development. More often that not, they were primarily mechanisms for determining pay. The role of the manager was very much to sit in judgement, and the subordinate was often lucky to get a word in edgeways. Worst of all, judgements were often made not on what had been achieved, but on the personality of the subordinate. Typically, managers were asked to tick boxes which rated the subordinate's leadership quality and so on. No help was provided to help the subordinate rectify some of the perceived weaknesses, and such appraisals were often a humiliating experience.

SECOND-GENERATION APPRAISAL

By the 1970s this rather autocratic approach to appraisal had been discredited, and replaced by a second generation of appraisal systems. Here the emphasis is on two-way communication. Both the manager ('the appraiser') and the subordinate ('the appraisee') are expected to play an equal role in the discussion. The appraisal meeting is intended as a frank and helpful review of the appraisee's work over the past year, a chance to set fresh objectives for the year ahead and to discuss what kinds of training and development will help the appraisee to achieve these objectives. Since the primary purpose of the appraisal is development, not assessment, discussions of pay are usually left to another occasion.

Second-generation appraisal has a great deal going for it – staff often feel that the chance to have an uninterrupted discussion with the boss for an hour or two is useful in itself. It's good to receive feedback from your manager, especially if it is positive. As we have seen, giving and receiving feedback is essential to building high trust relationships, so setting aside some time for this to happen in a well-thought-out way is a good use of time. Finally, appraisal makes time for a serious discussion of training and development – a topic which everyone seems to think is important, but which is often overlooked in the hurlyburly of everyday work.

In fact, appraisal was for a time seen as the great panacea, a cure for all organizational problems. So much so that in the 1980s and 1990s the British government put pressure on public sector bodies of all kinds to introduce appraisal systems, in the belief that it would somehow magically inject into them that elusive quality of 'business efficiency'.

The problem with second-generation appraisal systems is that they are heavily dependent on the interpersonal skills of the people leading them – the appraisers. If the appraiser takes a lot of trouble to find out how the appraisee is really doing, and if the appraiser is skilled enough to deliver this feedback

effectively, and if the appraiser is then prepared to
devote his or her time and the organization's money to
enable the appraisee to develop, then second-
generation systems work well. But these are some pretty
major ifs, and in many cases appraisers simply aren't up
to the mark.

What does your manager really know about how you do
your job? Unless you and your manager happen to work
alongside each other in the same room, the answer is
probably not very much. It shouldn't really be that
important. The success of your organization – and
ultimately your job security – depends less on the
perceptions you and your boss share, more on what your
customers think and do.

*Does your manager really
know?*

Perhaps the biggest drawback of second-generation
appraisal is the extent to which it fails to deliver on
training and development. This aspect of appraisal can
be a major selling point when attempting to introduce
appraisal to an unwilling workforce, whose only
experience may have been the humiliation of a first-
generation system. Indeed, appraisal systems are often
not called appraisal at all, but 'professional development
and review' or 'staff development and planning', in an
attempt to emphasize the training and development
aspect of the process. Expectations are raised, and when
they are not fulfilled trust leaves the office and cynicism
comes in to sit at its place. Why do second-generation
systems fail to deliver on development? Because training
and development are important, but rarely urgent.
Managers often feel under pressure to deliver short-term
results, rather than building long-term capability.

False expectations

The response to these criticisms of appraisal has been the
development of a third generation of appraisal systems,
popularly known as 360° appraisal.

**THIRD-GENERATION
APPRAISAL – THE 360°
APPROACH**

360° APPRAISAL AT EXXON CHEMICALS

Exxon Chemicals was one of the first companies to introduce 360° appraisals. With 14,000 employees, it is the third largest petrochemical company in the world. In 1993 it introduced 360° appraisal for 6000 managers working in 23 countries.

In preparation for his or her annual appraisal, each employee chooses eight 'knowledgeable others'. There must be a representative spread of team members (either senior or junior to the employee), customers (either internal or external) and peers. Each of these knowledgeable others completes a form, which asks for ratings and comments on 15 dimensions including commitment to quality, teamwork and effective communication. Because these dimensions are all observable behaviour, the feedback is useful. The forms, which usually take about 30 minutes to fill in, are returned to the employee's manager. The person completing the form has the option of returning it confidentially, although in practice about 90 per cent of the forms are returned with a signature.

At the appraisal meeting, the manager discusses the feedback from the knowledgeable others with the employee, and this forms the basis of the employee's development plan for the coming year.

Exxon Chemicals has found significant benefits in this approach to appraisal. One of its corporate goals is to 'maximize employee satisfaction' and employee surveys have shown that this has increased significantly since the introduction of 360° appraisal. There has been 100 per cent commitment to this method of appraisal. When Exxon first introduced it, there were concerns that the national cultures of some of the countries where it operates – Japan, Korea, Singapore – might not be conducive to a system which invites criticism of more senior staff. To the company's surprise, 360° appraisal works as well in these countries as anywhere else, perhaps because of a strong commitment to quality in the manufacturing ethos of these countries.

Although Exxon Chemicals' experience has been very positive, what works well for one organization may not work for another. There were certain aspects of Exxon's organizational culture which made it ready for 360° appraisal. The company had been taking a systematic approach to quality for many years. Employees were used to measuring quality in all its aspects, and welcomed a more systematic approach to measuring and developing human skills. Over 80 per cent of staff work in multi-level teams, so staff are familiar with the practice of exchanging feedback with both senior and junior staff. Most importantly, the overall level of trust in the organization is high, and staff are happy to give and receive quite personal feedback knowing that this information will not be misused.

Exxon Chemicals' approach to 360° appraisal may be described as an open system, in that those people giving feedback are happy to be known to the person receiving it. Many organizations have opted for a confidential system. People give feedback anonymously and the results are pooled, often by someone outside the company, before they are fed back to the individual concerned.

This is the approach taken by the Skipton Building Society, based in the north of England. Individuals choose who will be giving them feedback, and a form is sent to each of these. The questionnaires invite the respondents to comment on both the importance of a given competency to the job role concerned, as well as individual behaviour. The completed forms are sent directly to an outside consultancy, which collates the information and returns it to the person from the human resource department who will be helping people make sense of all this feedback.

The linchpin of the whole process is the moment the individual receives the feedback. Most people are unused to receiving such an intense dose of feedback. Some may find it shocking, others may find it a very pleasant surprise. It is vital that this meeting is led by someone with considerable interpersonal skills. Once the individual has received feedback from a trained HR person, he or she prepares a personal development plan. This is discussed at a three-way meeting between the individual, the manager and the HR person. This ensures that there is commitment from the individual, support from the manager and resources from the organization to make sure that development happens.

Does the system work? Out of 180 requests for feedback in its first year of operation, only one person failed to give feedback. In a recent staff attitude survey, 84 per cent said that they felt the society genuinely cared about their development. Staff turnover is very low, and this is all the more remarkable when you consider that major competitors – the Halifax and the Bradford & Bingley – are headquartered nearby. The Skipton has shown increases in profits for the last three successive years.

Implementing a third-generation appraisal system is not easy – the prospect of asking a wide range of your working colleagues to comment on your abilities is not one most people automatically embrace with open arms. What did the Skipton do to ensure such a smooth implementation? Training manager Cherry House explains:

> The culture of the organization as a whole is very important. Because we are relatively small and staff turnover is so low, many staff consider their colleagues as friends. Our chief executive, John Goodfellow, does a lot to promote a high trust environment – he walks the job, eats in the staff canteen, introduces every induction course and sales conference, and visits branches a lot. He's also very committed to training. So far as the 360° appraisal is concerned, we wouldn't have gone straight into it cold. We've been using

development centres for a few years now, and so we were able to pilot the 360° idea there. When we did introduce it we were very careful to brief everyone involved beforehand.

Personnel director Ian Walker agrees with this analysis, and adds another important factor:

Staff were a bit reticent about the 360° idea at first. But they trusted Cherry as a person. Staff felt that if Cherry said it would be handled fairly, then it would be.

Even if your organization does not have a 360° feedback system, you can still introduce the principles behind it into more traditional appraisal systems.

WHAT IF YOU'RE NOT THE CEO OR THE HR DIRECTOR?

- In advance of being appraised, seek feedback on your performance from key working relationships. Having an appraisal gives you an excellent reason to ask.

- Before you lead the next appraisal of your staff, point out to them that you may not be the best person to give them feedback. Ask them to identify the people whose feedback really matters to them, and agree how this information could be brought to the appraisal meeting.

Promote Learning 10

Trust is the highest form of human motivation. It brings out the very best in people. But it takes time and patience, and it doesn't preclude the necessity to train and develop people so that their competency can rise to the level of that trust.

Stephen Covey

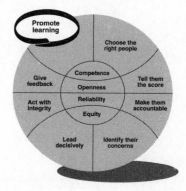

*I*F you want to build a high trust organization, you want your people to be competent. But choosing competent people to join you is not enough. Skills and knowledge rapidly become outdated in a fast-changing world. People remain competent only if they are committed to **learning**.

Nowhere is change faster than in the computing industry. Have you ever bought one of those greetings cards that plays 'Happy Birthday' when you open it up? It contains more electronic computing power than existed in the whole world before 1950. A home video camera has more processing power than the IBM 360, the wonder machine that gave birth to the mainframe computing age. In fact, if there had been the same rate of progress in the automotive industry as there has been in computers, you would now be able to buy a Rolls-Royce for £2 and it would travel at the speed of sound for 600 miles on a thimbleful of petrol.

It's not just computer businesses which are fast changing – new technology affects almost every business. Writers Stan Davis and Jim Botkin estimate that the world's total knowledge doubles about every seven years. Much of what students learn on a three-year degree course is out of date by the time they graduate. There's only one way to stay competent in such a maelstrom, and that's to be extraordinarily good at the business of learning.

Not so long ago, training and development were something done to the people low down in the company. It was fine for new recruits and shopfloor staff to be trained, but not for middle and senior managers. Ten years ago, a number of reports appeared which concluded that managers' commitment to training in the UK was too little, too late. One of these reports, by Charles Handy, found that over half of UK companies made no formal provision at all for the training of managers. But the situation is changing. A 1997 study by the Open University found that over 96 per cent of large companies and 80 per cent of small companies now provide training for managers. Similar attention is being paid to development in the best organizations across the world.

Even the most senior staff are finding it necessary to take learning seriously. Starbucks' CEO Howard Schultz describes how important learning was to him as his coffee company continued to expand:

> Can a company double and even triple in size but stay true to its values? How far can you extend a brand before you dilute it? How do you innovate without compromising your legacy? How do you stay entrepreneurial even as you develop professional management? How do you keep pushing through on long-term initiatives when short-term problems demand immediate attention? How do you continue to

provide customers with a sense of discovery when you are growing at the speed of light? How do you maintain the company's soul when you also need systems and processes?

With no easy answers, I explored every avenue I could find. I've always been a voracious reader, but now I began to read even more widely. I consulted experts. I got to know other CEOs and entrepreneurs. I hired managers who had done it before. I picked the brains of everyone I met: reporters, analysts, investors, store managers, staff, customers.

Without learning, there is no competence; without competence there is no trust. In some cases, without competence there is no company either, because it has been wiped out by competition. That's why a commitment to learning – your own and for others – is an essential practice in the high trust organization.

HOW TO LEARN

Whenever you learn anything, you go through a sequence of four states. To begin with you are unaware that you need to learn. You may not be doing something terribly well, but you just don't realize. This is a state of **unconscious incompetence**. Then something happens which brings to your attention the fact that you're not doing whatever it is very well. Somebody else might tell you, or you might figure out that something isn't quite right. You're still not doing it well, but now you *know* you're not doing it well. This is a state of **conscious incompetence**.

The next step is to do something about this lack of skill – to take part in some kind of learning activity. There are many to choose from and we'll look at them in detail later in this chapter. So you learn the skill – you have reached the state of **conscious competence**. Conscious competence is hard work. Like a child who has just learned to walk, you have to think carefully about each step, otherwise you tumble over. Of course, children soon learn to walk without thinking consciously about where to put each foot – they do it unconsciously. The final state in the learning process is **unconscious competence**.

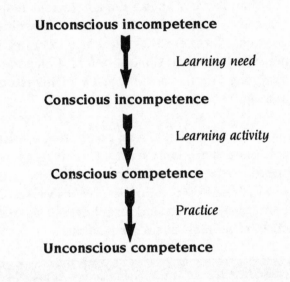

Unconscious incompetence

Learning need

Conscious incompetence

Learning activity

Conscious competence

Practice

Unconscious competence

In order to move from unconscious incompetence to conscious incompetence, you have to identify what it is you need to learn. To move from conscious incompetence to conscious competence, you need to choose the most appropriate learning activity. To move from conscious competence to unconscious competence, you need practice. Let's look at each of these in turn.

IDENTIFY YOUR LEARNING NEED

● What are your company's objectives and values?

● What tasks do you need to carry out in order to contribute to your company's success? What specific resources would help you to achieve these tasks? What skills and knowledge would be useful to you?

● What are the concerns of the people you need to be

able to trust? What skills would help you to address their concerns?

● What decisions do you need to make? What skills and knowledge would help you with these decisions?

● How can you, your team and your company honour promises and maintain a reputation for reliability? What skills would help?

One of the most powerful ways in which we can become aware of our learning needs is by seeking feedback, as discussed in the previous chapter. In fact, excellent learners are addicted to feedback – they just can't get enough information about the effects of their behaviour. What's more, they're not bothered by what might appear to be a failure – to them, this is useful information. RW Johnson, former CEO of Johnson & Johnson, once said: 'Failure is our most important product.' He meant that a willingness to learn what didn't work was an essential part of the process of finding what did.

CHOOSE A LEARNING ACTIVITY

Have you ever attended a training course which you thought was marvellous, only to find that a colleague was lukewarm about it? Have you ever raved over a particular book and insisted someone else read it, only to find it bored them? Or vice versa? People are different and we learn differently.

According to psychologist David Kolb, there are four essential elements in any learning activity. We have to **do** the activity we want to be competent at; we have to **look** at what we've done; we have to **think** how to do it better; and we have to **plan** how to do it differently next time. These four stages of doing, looking, thinking and planning form a learning cycle (see Figure 3). The more times we loop around this cycle, the better we get.

But where do you begin? Some people have a strong

The learning cycle

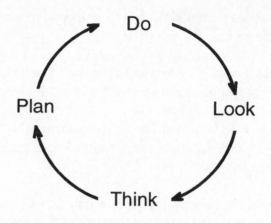

Figure 3   The learning cycle

preference for beginning at the practical end – by doing or looking. Others have a strong preference for beginning at the more theoretical end – by thinking or planning. It's worth knowing what your preference is. You might as well choose learning activities that make learning easy for you, rather than those which make it hard.

One week I found myself leading a training course on the same topic for two very different organizations – an oil exploration company and a university. The subject matter – teamwork – was similar for both groups, but the way I presented it was very different. The managers in the oil company had a strong preference for beginning their learning with practical activities. The course was full of role plays and other practical tasks. This was a group of managers who loved rolling up their sleeves and getting their hands dirty. The university academics were completely the opposite – before they could do anything, they needed to have a good theoretical grasp of the underlying concepts. I gave them a course brimming with research, models and theories. They loved it. Both groups learned a lot, but in their own way.

Another useful distinction in learning preferences is between people who learn best in groups, and those who learn best alone. Most of the academics on the teamwork course had a fine time debating the various research findings on what makes an effective team with the sharp analysis and vigour which academics love. But one participant was more restrained. When I asked him how he was finding the course, he was more interested in picking my brains about the book list I had included as part of the course materials – he was someone who learned more on his own than he did in groups.

Putting these distinctions – theory v practice and group v alone – on to the two axes of the matrix so beloved by management writers, we get the grid shown in Figure 4.

	Theory	**Practice**
Group	1. Training courses, seminars, conferences	2. Teambuilding 3. Working groups
Alone	6. Coaching, mentoring 7. Self-directed learning	4. Visits and job shadowing 5. Special projects, job rotation

Figure 4   Learning preferences

Before we examine each of these learning activities in turn, it's worth saying that this model is unhelpful if it is used too prescriptively. Just because I learn more easily in a group doesn't mean that reading a book will be a waste of time, or vice versa. In fact, most people are able to learn in most of the ways I've listed; it's just that some people learn better with some activities than with others. If you are serious about becoming an excellent learner, and an excellent promoter of learning, it's worth being curious about your preferences and how they may be different from other people's.

**TRAINING COURSES,
SEMINARS AND
CONFERENCES**

All high trust organizations believe in the value of formal training. They give new recruits a week or more of orientation training, which provides not only basic knowledge about the new employer, but an understanding of the key values which are so essential in a high trust environment. They also provide a full menu of skills-based training to existing staff. Some even have a corporate 'university'.

There is a great deal to be said for training courses: they are a focused way of bringing new skills and knowledge to a group of people. But there are drawbacks. It's tempting to use training courses in the same way as farmers dip their sheep – driving everyone through, whether they need it or not. Training courses lack the immediacy of some other learning methods – teaching someone out-of-date material is a waste of time. Most worrying of all, training is removed from the realities of the workplace. It takes a good trainer and a determined learner to make sure that the lessons can be applied back at work.

TEAMBUILDING

Strong teams are a common feature of high trust organizations. Organizing specific teambuilding events is a very effective way of notching up team performance.

What do teams need to learn? Successful teams are high trust teams, and so they need to be experts at the practices covered in this book. They need to have the right people; they need to share clear objectives and values; they need to know who does what, so that everyone knows what they are accountable for; individuals need to feel that their specific concerns are appreciated, and the team needs to find a way to make decisions which are trust enhancing. The team must act with integrity and honour its commitments. It must be good at feedback and learning.

One way of developing these practices within a team is to engage in activities which are very different from the team's usual work – making towers out of building blocks or abseiling down a cliff face. While this approach works for some people, it's not for everyone. More importantly, when Jon Katzenbach and Douglas Smith studied a whole range of teams for their book *The Wisdom of Teams*, they found that the highest performers rarely engaged in this kind of artificial activity at all. Instead, they concentrated their teambuilding efforts on real issues: setting challenging objectives and agreeing fundamental values, holding team members accountable for what they did and so on.

When a university merged its computer department with its library service this seemed a logical move. After all, both groups were involved in making information accessible. In practice, it was an unsettling experience for both sides, and nowhere was this more felt than in the management team whose job it was to lead the new department. When the newly appointed director of information services asked me to lead a teambuilding event for this new group, his first comment was: 'You're not going to make us do silly things with Lego bricks, are you?'

I didn't use Lego bricks at all. Instead, I encouraged the group to focus on what they were there to do, and how they were going to do it. The process was not always easy – some harsh words were exchanged over the respective cultures of the two former departments – but once the top team had a clear sense of what it was there to do, it was able to provide decisive leadership not only to the rest of the department, but to the university as a whole.

WORKING GROUPS

Bringing people together to form a temporary working group can also be a powerful vehicle for learning. Participants find out about each other's area of knowledge, form working relationships and learn more about working collaboratively. They can also come up with some great ideas for the company.

In 1990 Starbucks set up a working group, made up of people from across the company, to look at the broad topic of 'people growth'. The group was responsible for a number of significant innovations at the company. One of these is the mission review system. Any member of

Starbucks' staff can report any action taken by the company which appears to be in conflict with the objectives and values set out in its mission statement. Printed cards for this purpose are given to new recruits and are easily available in all work locations. If people choose to sign the card, they get a personal response. Even if they don't use their name, their comments are taken seriously.

VISITS AND JOB SHADOWING

If you really want to learn how to do something well, find someone who does it excellently and go and study them to see what makes the difference.

In the early 1980s, the US economy was in serious trouble. From cars to computers, US firms were being hammered by Japanese competition. As an NBC documentary of the time commented chillingly, 'This could be the first generation of Americans to enjoy a standard of living lower than their parents.' Droves of top US managers flocked to Japan to try to figure out what was going on. One of the companies which visited Japan to see what could be learned was aircraft maker Boeing. Like many of its US counterparts, Boeing learned a lot from those visits about manufacturing methods and the importance of a commitment to never-ending improvement. It also learned something else: the importance of trust. In *Company Man*, Anthony Sampson describes how Boeing had struggled from near bankruptcy in the 1970s to commercial success once again in the 1990s. The biggest obstacle, according to human resources director Larry McKean, was changing the attitudes of Boeing's 16,000 managers. Sampson asked McKean why it took so long to accept something which seems so obvious: that people work better when they are consulted and treated like adults. McKean replied sadly: 'Trust. We monitored them, supervised them, told them when to go to the bathroom. We didn't trust our own people.'

Visits don't have to be across continents to be useful. One theatre company I know saved itself from extinction simply by sending its marketing staff on a visit to another company a few hundred yards down the road. The place you visit doesn't even have to be in the same line of business for you to learn from it – in fact from the point of view of competition it's easier if it isn't. What you do need is a willingness to learn from other people. Some teams and organizations suffer from the 'not invented here' syndrome. Excellent learners take precisely the opposite approach – they delight in modelling themselves on others, creative swiping and copying good ideas.

Taking on a special project, above and beyond your everyday activity, is a very good way to learn. 3M has institutionalized this way of learning as one of its core values. All technical staff are expected to spend 15 per cent of their time pursuing projects of their own choosing and initiative. Many, of course, are resounding failures commercially – but a few are sufficiently successful for the company to prosper.

SPECIAL PROJECTS AND JOB ROTATION

Taking on not just a project but a whole new job is another good way of learning. Many large corporations routinely rotate people around jobs. Some use job rotation for their new recruits, others may also have a systematic programme of developing people by moving them from job to job. At its best, job rotation has many benefits. It encourages the spread of different outlooks, ideas and perspectives throughout the company. It enables individuals to have experiences that they wouldn't be able to have any other way. It also encourages managers to build self-sustaining teams.

While there is a great deal to be said for this approach, there are drawbacks. There is no doubt that the people who move from job to job usually learn a lot. But what about the people who don't? One multinational company assesses all its new recruits within a few months of joining, and decides how far they have the potential to progress. Those who have a low rating are given plodding jobs and generally stay there. Those who are assessed as high flyers change jobs every few years and rapidly ascend the corporate ladder. Does the system work? Or is it just a self-fulfilling prophecy? What is sure is that the high flyers leave a wake of resentment and mistrust behind them as they go. One manager commented to me:

> The thing about the high flyers is that the company believes they can do no wrong. Because they don't get a chance to understand each new job properly, they can make some big mistakes. It doesn't matter to them because they'll soon be moving on to another job. Those of us left behind have to clear up the mess.

High trust organizations do use special projects and job rotation, but they put the onus on the individual to make the project work to everyone's benefit. Semco encourages its managers to move around jobs, and in a given year about a quarter of all managers do. As with most other programmes at Semco, this isn't organized centrally but left to individual initiative. In addition, once a year, Semco chooses one young person from its new recruits and gives them no job description, no set responsibilities and no boss. They are free to roam the company as they wish and do whatever they want, provided that they work in at least 12 different departments. Their only accountability is that they have to generate enough revenue to cover their salary costs. Semco calls this approach 'Lost in Space'. At the end of 12 months, the person is free to negotiate a more permanent arrangement with any of the departments in which they've served.

COACHING AND MENTORING

Semco's 'Lost in Space' programme may seem an unusual way to treat new recruits, but WL Gore treats all its new people in a very similar way. New associates look around the company and find a place where they can make a contribution. But they are not completely on their own. Each new associate is assigned a sponsor, who takes a personal interest in the new associate's contributions, goals and problems. The sponsor serves as advocate, friend and coach. As time goes on, associates may acquire other sponsors. In fact, it is common for people who have been with the company for a while to have a number of sponsors.

You don't need to work in a company like WL Gore to benefit from this approach to learning. Any organization can offer coaching and mentoring to its staff. The two terms are sometimes used interchangeably, but it is useful to make a distinction. **Coaching** focuses on particular tasks – how to achieve production targets, how to get your team to trust each other. **Mentoring** is more concerned with the longer term – how do I want my career to unfold, and what can I do now to make this happen? It's common for coaching to be provided by your immediate manager, and for mentoring to come from someone else, but it doesn't necessarily have to be that way. The most productive coaching and mentoring relationships are going to be with people you trust, whatever your formal relationship in terms of the organizational structure.

In a sense, skimming the business pages of your newspaper could be viewed as self-directed learning, but the term is usually taken to mean something a little more systematic. The main resources for self-directed learning are:

**SELF-DIRECTED
LEARNING**

- books and journals

- audiotapes, plus workbooks

- videotapes, plus workbooks

- computer-based training.

Many companies make these resources available to staff in an open learning centre, either to borrow for use in their own time or to use at the centre itself.

RR Donnelley & Sons, with 38,000 employees, is the largest printing company in the US. Its East Plant churns out millions of copies of TV *Guide*, *Reader's Digest* and the *New York Times Magazine*. Following the lead of Jack Stack's SRC, RR Donnelley chose this plant in which to introduce open book management. As a way of teaching employees about finances, the company asked a software house to develop a computer-based business simulation game. Called Celestial Cheese, the game invites players to manage a fanciful but highly realistic business, with very similar characteristics to Donnelley's printing business. Employees are encouraged to play the game at home, in breaks and during downtime at the plant. Once they have mastered the fictional game, they are invited to play similar games, but this time with the real company. One game focused on the need to improve throughput in the gravure pressroom, and a computer fed back the results of employee decisions. The very first run of the game saved the company $26,000.

Computer-based training is a particularly useful way of learning to deal with situations which occur too rarely in real life for you to learn 'on the job', but which are too costly to recreate on a training course. When a fire broke out at London's Notting Hill carnival, it was quickly contained by the London Fire Brigade, despite the logistical problems of taking large fire appliances through an area thronged with people. The officer in charge explained that he had already dealt with an almost identical problem as part of a computer-based simulation.

PRACTICE

The right learning activity can help you to learn a skill in the same way that driving lessons can help you to learn how to drive a car. But you will never be a really skilful driver if you have to think consciously 'Now's the time to apply the brake' every time you want to slow down. In order to be really skilful, you need to have unconscious competence. In other words, you need to be able to act skilfully without consciously thinking what it is you are doing. Without unconscious competence, a whole raft of human activities would either be impossible or could only be done at painfully slow speeds – playing a musical instrument, typing at a computer keyboard, playing most sports. The same applies to business. If you had to think consciously every time you opened your mouth 'Should I ask a closed or an open question at this point?', you wouldn't be much of a communicator.

When we talk about intuition, we are often referring simply to our unconscious competence at making good judgements. Have you ever felt on meeting someone that you couldn't trust them, even though there was nothing specific that you could put your finger on? This is your intuition – your unconscious competence – at work. You may even have gone on and trusted the person, because there was no rational reason not to. The chances are that you were disappointed, however. It's worth listening to your intuition, but not trusting it regardless. Even your intuition can be wrong sometimes.

Intuition

How do you develop unconscious competence? The same way you get to be really good at playing a sport or a musical instrument – by practice. The more you do, the better you will get, provided of course that you continue to get the kind of feedback which enables you to do better, not just to repeat your mistakes over and over again.

That's why training courses can sometimes be such a letdown – you don't get the chance to practise the new skills you have learned. So whenever you learn a new skill, make sure that you give yourself lots of opportunities to practise it. It may seem corny and old fashioned, but the main reason some people get really good at some things is because they do them a lot.

THE BELIEFS OF LEARNING

If you want to be trustworthy, you need to be competent. If you want to be competent you need to be good at learning. If you want to be good at learning, you need to know what to learn, you need to choose an appropriate learning activity and you need to practise. But all this is not enough. You need to have a set of beliefs which will enable you to learn.

Above all else, get **curious**. Curiosity is without doubt

the most useful mindset to have when it comes to learning. The world's great thinkers have all been curious (often in both senses of the word). Einstein was curious about what it would be like if you could travel at the speed of light, and this led him to his theory of relativity. Darwin was curious as to why there were so many different kinds of creatures roaming the earth, and this led him to his theories about evolution.

Curiosity drives most successful businesspeople too. Akio Morita and Masura Ibuka, Sony's co-founders, got curious about how small you could make electrical products – and so the Walkman was born. Spencer Silver at 3M was curious about a glue he'd devised that wouldn't stick properly. Arthur Fry, also at 3M, was curious to solve the problem he had with his hymnbook at church – whenever he picked it up he always seemed to lose the scraps of paper he used to mark the pages of that morning's hymns. When Silver and Fry got together, the Post-it note was born.

Curiosity is not only good for learning, it is in itself a great trust builder. If you run your life on relationships based on power, you're not going to be curious at all. If someone breaks their part of the bargain, you'll apply whatever sanctions you think are appropriate, end of story. If you base relationships on hope, you'll just accept what happens, come what may. But if you want to build relationships on trust, you'll be curious about other people's behaviour. You won't take things for granted and you'll be less likely to jump to conclusions. In these circumstances, trust will thrive.

AN ENVIRONMENT FOR LEARNING

What kind of working environment best promotes learning? Being surrounded by other people who are curious certainly helps. Having appropriate systems is important too. The best kind of performance appraisal systems aren't just concerned with giving feedback and setting new goals – they are also mechanisms for promoting learning. Some organizations also use a system of personal learning plans. Individual members of staff are encouraged to set out on paper their individual learning objectives and to be systematic about achieving them.

More than this, high trust organizations have the kind of culture which is never content with today's standards, which always wants to find a better way. Of course they want to do better than their competitors. Even if they are number one in their field, that's not good enough. Good enough never is. They always want to be **beating their own records**. First Direct isn't content with 15,000 new customers a month – it wants to improve that rate. Each Wal-Mart store compares its daily performance with the same day one year ago. The aim, of course, is to get better year on year. Motorola has abandoned some markets altogether – television and car radios, for example – not because they were unprofitable, but as a way of forcing the company to look for something better. 3M's rule that each division of the company must make 30 per cent of its sales from products introduced in the previous four years fulfils a similar function.

Better and better

Many organizations pay lip service to the idea of continuous improvement, but not so many put it into practice. The reason is that they are not usually willing to take the risk of trying something different. Organizations which are comfortable with **risk taking** are going to promote a lot of learning. Organizations which value conformity are not going to see very much learning. High trust companies are very comfortable with risk taking. Their attitude is to try something and see if it works. It doesn't matter if they get it wrong a lot of the time, because the times they get it right will amply repay the risk. In this sense high trust organizations are more like organisms, evolving to adapt to a changing environment. Low trust organizations are more like machines, insisting that exactly the right part is put in to fix any problems.

Take risks

Isn't there a contradiction between this willingness to take risks and the toughness which high trust organizations exercise when it comes to getting results? The two go hand in hand, and this is how. **High trust organizations are tough on results and they are tough on values.** And values are always more important than short-term results because it's adherence to values which creates the long-term results. If an employee takes some risks, but does so in the framework of the company's values, that's fine, even if the short-term consequences are not good.

Nordstrom sales associate Van Mensah received a letter from a Swedish customer who had recently purchased a large quantity of shirts. The letter said that when the customer washed the shirts in hot water, they all shrank. Mensah called the customer in Sweden and said that he would replace the shirts free of charge – even though the washing instructions clearly stated that a cool wash was needed. Mensah was taking a risk: by sending new shirts to a customer when the company was in no way at fault, he was in effect harming Nordstrom's profits and his own sales bonus. But he knew that the risk was worth taking because it was so in line with the company's dedication to customer service. He commented:

> I knew that I would never be blamed for doing too much for a customer, but I might get in trouble for doing too little.

High trust organizations know that learning is so important to trust and survival that it is often an explicit part of their corporate values. 3M, First Direct, Hewlett-Packard, Johnson & Johnson, Leyland Trucks, Marks & Spencer, Motorola, Nordstrom, Northern Foods, SRC, Sony, Wal-Mart all have a commitment to learning and continuous improvement at the heart of their corporate ideology. This means that they continue to spend time and money on training and development, even when the environment is difficult. In fact, they may spend more in the lean times because they believe that this is the best way to make things better.

Coda

Next Steps *11*

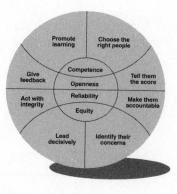

*R*EADING a book about trust isn't enough to create trust in your workplace. You also have to take action. This concluding chapter is designed to help you make the transition between learning some new ideas and putting them into practice.

But first remember that you won't be able to trust other people, or persuade them to trust you, unless and until you trust **yourself**.

WHAT DO YOU WANT?

Take a few moments to think about your workplace. Focus your thoughts on the part of it you have most influence over. If you are the chief executive, you may want to consider the whole organization. If not, you'll find it most useful to think about your department or team. Now: what would it be like if there were the highest possible levels of trust in working relationships? Take a few moments to think, even to daydream, about what this would be like. How would people interact with each other? What would you see? What would you hear? What would this feel like?

When you've given yourself the time you need to think, write it down in the box below.

Now let me ask you this. Have you described your ideal high trust environment in positive terms? Or have you described it in terms of what people will *not* be doing? You're more likely to get what you want if you express your aspirations in positive language. So if you've used phrases like 'people wouldn't argue so much', please rephrase this in a positive way, such as 'people would work together more harmoniously'.

Another important question about what you've written: is it consistent with your own set of values and beliefs? If, for example, you've described how your team would be happily beavering away without interference from you, but one of your core beliefs is that you exist to hold the whole team together, then clearly there is inconsistency. Read what you've written again. If your intuition tells you that something is not quite right, amend your statement until it's something that you would be happy about. Don't worry if you're not yet clear how to achieve this wonderful state of affairs; just be sure that you would be genuinely happy with it if you could bring it about.

MAKING PROGRESS

You know what you want to achieve. Now think for a moment: what would your workplace be like if you were halfway to achieving this desired state? Please write this in the box below. Again, express it positively and make sure that it is consistent with your own values and beliefs.

STARTING

You know what the halfway point is like. Now think: what are the three areas you need to address, in order to move towards your halfway point, and eventually to your desired state? Write them in the box overleaf.

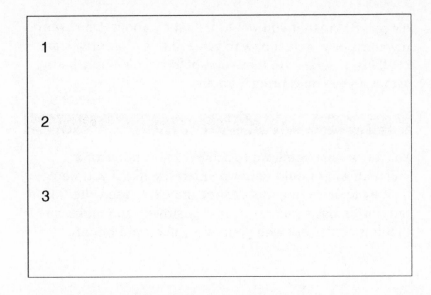

If you need a break, now's a good time to have one…

ANALYSIS

Having put some thought into where you want to be, let's do some analysis of where you are now. To what extent do you demonstrate the behaviours listed below? Score yourself 1 – not at all, 2 – a little, 3 – quite a bit, 4 – a great deal, 5 – almost all the time. Better still, ask a work colleague to give you his or her assessment of you, using the same questionnaire.

To what extent do I…

CHOOSE THE RIGHT PEOPLE

Know in advance what I am looking for in a new member of staff

      1   2   3   4   5

Have a good track record of recruiting excellent new staff

      1   2   3   4   5

Ask perceptive questions of potential new recruits

      1   2   3   4   5

Give fair treatment to all candidates

      1   2   3   4   5

Talk about the company's objectives

      1   2   3   4   5

Live by the company's values

      1   2   3   4   5

Educate others about the company's objectives and values

      1   2   3   4   5

Get motivated by more than money

      1   2   3   4   5

TELL THEM THE SCORE

Judge accurately the competence of others

      1   2   3   4   5

Explain clearly what I expect of others

      1   2   3   4   5

Let people get on without interference

      1   2   3   4   5

Get tough on people who do not produce results

      1   2   3   4   5

MAKE THEM ACCOUNTABLE

Spend time listening to others

      1   2   3   4   5

Get out and about

      1   2   3   4   5

Make myself very approachable

      1   2   3   4   5

Listen perceptively

      1   2   3   4   5

IDENTIFY THEIR CONCERNS

LEAD DECISIVELY

Make decisions which others consider equitable

   1   2   3   4   5

Consult others to an appropriate degree

   1   2   3   4   5

Find win/win solutions to problems

   1   2   3   4   5

Communicate adequately the result of decisions

   1   2   3   4   5

ACT WITH INTEGRITY

Keep my promises

   1   2   3   4   5

Act proactively

   1   2   3   4   5

Act consistently

   1   2   3   4   5

Have high ethical standards

   1   2   3   4   5

GIVE FEEDBACK

Tell people when they've done a good job

   1   2   3   4   5

Give useful criticism

   1   2   3   4   5

Deliver criticism sensitively

   1   2   3   4   5

Accept feedback

   1   2   3   4   5

PROMOTE LEARNING

Want to do better

   1   2   3   4   5

Engage in learning activities

      1   2   3   4   5

Share new ideas with others

      1   2   3   4   5

Work hard to develop new skills

      1   2   3   4   5

Once you have completed this questionnaire, think about what it tells you. Which aspects of building the trust effect do you need to work on?

PRACTICAL ACTIONS

You know where you want to go to, you know where you are now. What practical steps are you going to take to get there? In the box below, write down three specific trust-enhancing actions which you will take this week. If you are stuck for ideas, refer to the list which follows the box.

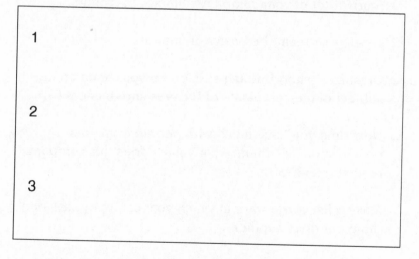

1

2

3

❑ Next time you meet someone for the first time, note whether your intuition is to trust them or not.

CHOOSE THE RIGHT
PEOPLE

❑ Draw up a person specification for the next post you recruit under the three headings of technical skills, people skills and attitudes/values.

❑ Next time you interview someone for a job, ask them to make a short presentation.

❑ Next time you interview someone for a job, say to them: please tell me a story which illustrates your ability to…

❑ At your next one-to-one business meeting, make a mental note – is the other person fast paced or slow paced?

❑ Watch people at meetings and conferences. When people are engaged in conversation, do their body postures match or clash?

TELL THEM THE SCORE

❑ Make an opportunity to ask your CEO what he or she considers to be the company's purpose and objectives.

❑ Study a set of your company's financial accounts.

❑ Teach your team the basics of finance.

❑ Organize a short briefing session for your team on the subject of the company's objectives and finances.

❑ Next time you have lunch with people from your organization, ask them: what values does this company really believe in?

❑ Make a list of the ways in which your company says one thing but does another.

MAKE THEM ACCOUNTABLE

❑ Assess each member of your team in terms of skills and commitment.

❑ Use the OPERA model next time you delegate any task.

❑ Identify one area where you are supervising staff too closely and stop.

❑ Identify one petty rule or regulation and dispense with it.

❑ At your next team meeting announce that you will be holding staff more accountable for what they do – and explain what this means.

❑ Arrange to meet one of your suppliers simply to get to know him or her better.

❑ Set yourself a quantitative goal for listening to people.

IDENTIFY THEIR CONCERNS

❑ The next time you start to write a memo, phone instead.

❑ The next conversation you have, make it your sole outcome to find out what the other person thinks.

❑ Identify one business relationship where you habitually meet at your place, not theirs. Arrange to meet at theirs next time.

❑ Identify one business relationship where you haven't talked to the person involved for over three months. Give them a call.

❑ Go and work alongside one of your team members or suppliers for a day.

❑ Think of a bad decision you've made recently. Make an opportunity to apologize to the people involved.

LEAD DECISIVELY

❑ The next time you are faced with a decision which affects other people, sit down for 10 minutes and weigh up the relative merits of decide and sell, negotiate, propose and consult, and blank sheet consultation.

❑ The next negotiation you are involved in, identify one thing that you and the other party can agree on.

❑ The next time you consult with staff, use a document with at least three headings: what has already been decided; what is open to change; the mechanics of the consultation process.

❑ The next major decision you have to implement, pilot it first.

❑ Make sure that you communicate the outcome of your next major decision in at least three ways: direct to all staff; on paper; via managers and team leaders.

ACT WITH INTEGRITY

❑ For one week, keep a time log of how you spend each 15 minutes of your working day.

❑ Make only specific, time-based promises; not 'I'll try to do my best', but 'I'll do it next Wednesday'.

❑ If you are know you are going to break a promise, contact the person and apologize in advance.

❑ Whenever you face a dilemma, act as if you had a lot of choices.

❑ Write your own obituary – at least the one you would like to be written about you.

❑ Whenever you feel in an ethical dilemma, ask yourself: what if everyone concerned knew about this?

GIVE FEEDBACK

❑ Next time someone gives you some praise, listen to it.

❑ Next time someone gives you some criticism, ask them to make it as specific as possible.

❑ Just before you give someone feedback, check with your intuition: is this person ready right now to take in what I have to say?

❑ Get agreement at a team meeting that everyone will give and receive more feedback, providing it is behavioural.

❑ The next time you have some important feedback to give, rehearse it first with a friend, to make sure you are giving behávioural feedback.

❑ Next time you are involved with a performance appraisal, make sure that it's not just based on the views of the appraiser and the appraisee. Bring in other people's perspectives as well.

❑ Identify one skill that is crucial to your job. Ask an appropriate person for some feedback on your performance in this area.

PROMOTE LEARNING

❑ Ask three colleagues to tell you about the best training course they've ever attended. Make sure you attend a comparable event this year.

❑ Choose one book from the list in the bibliography. Buy it and read it.

❑ Volunteer for, or set up, some kind of company-wide working group.

❑ Arrange to visit another company from which you could learn something useful.

❑ If you could have anyone in your company as a mentor, who would it be? Go and ask him or her to be your mentor.

Every time you use an idea from this list, tick it off. Keep coming back to the list until you have done them all.

A KEY RELATIONSHIP

So far in this chapter I've invited you to consider a whole range of actions which would contribute towards a high trust workplace. I now want you to get very specific indeed – to focus on just one working relationship. As I said right at the beginning of the book, great organizations are not made up of great people – they are made up of great **relationships** between people. Consider all the working relationships you are engaged in – with your bosses and your subordinates, lateral relationships across the organization, with suppliers, partners and customers, both outside and inside the organization. If you had to choose just one relationship where an improvement in the levels of trust would make a big difference, which relationship would it be? Write it here:

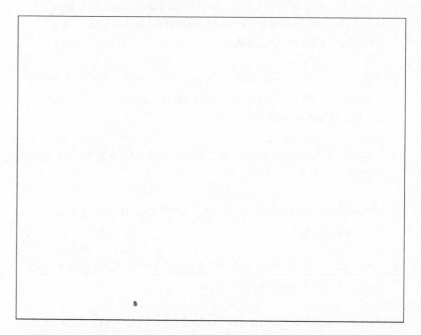

Before you do some work to make the relationship better, I want you to answer this question: how bad does it have to get before you end the relationship? Write your answer opposite.

If you find it hard to answer this question immediately, that's OK – in some circumstances it is a very tough question indeed. If you can't answer it straight away, continue with the rest of the activity for now – but do return to it.

Your first step is to get curious about why trust is currently lacking. What's your assessment of this person in terms of the CORE of the trust effect – competence, openness, reliability and equity? In the box below, score them high, medium or low on each of these areas, adding any comments you need to.

Competence	High	Medium	Low
Openness	High	Medium	Low
Reliability	High	Medium	Low
Equity	High	Medium	Low

Now step into their shoes – what would be their assessment of you?

Competence	High	Medium	Low
Openness	High	Medium	Low
Reliability	High	Medium	Low
Equity	High	Medium	Low

Imagine that you can see these two people – yourself and the other person – from a distance. Imagine you are watching them on a video recording or in a movie. How do you feel about the way they relate to each other? What's going on? What would help?

Now mentally step back into your own shoes again. What three specific actions could *you* do to improve the level of trust in this relationship? Write them here:

1

2

3

Now do them!

TALKING TO OTHERS

Think of one other person who might be interested in the topic of trust in organizations. If they asked you why trust is important to your organization right now, what would you say? Write the key points of your answer in the box below.

TRUSTING YOURSELF

Imagine a flock of birds, wheeling and turning together in the sky as they group for their annual migration. Hear the sound of their wings beating the air, and recall for a moment your feeling of amazement at the sight. Hundreds, even thousands of birds fly in a formation that changes shape and direction as it moves. In order to do this, each bird must fly slightly differently to its neighbour – as the formation changes direction, for example, those birds on the outside must fly more quickly than those in the middle. It is both beautiful and purposeful – it prepares the flock for the awesome task of flying almost continuously for thousands of miles on their migratory trek.

Some organizations are like this. By harnessing the power of the trust effect, these organizations are able to perform gracefully and economically.

Now contrast this, if you will, with a flock of sheep being driven to new pastures. They amble along, bleating plaintively, rubbing shoulders with each other. Without the encouragement of the farmer or the sheepdogs urging them on, they are just as likely to stop wherever they are. Every so often one or two sheep will make a break for freedom, only to be brought back again by the sheepdogs, ever obedient to the farmer's will. Progress is slow and ungainly.

Some organizations are like flocks of sheep. Staff don't seem to know where they are going or why, and without the constant encouragement of their managers – the sheepdogs – there is a danger that things will grind to a halt. Even so, staff will occasionally go right off course, and it is the manager's job to bring them back, as the sheepdogs reclaim the lost sheep. The chief executive is like the farmer – in overall control but utterly dependent on his or her managers to get anything done at all. Progress is slow and ungainly.

What would you rather be – a sheep or a bird?

Bibliography

Adams, Scott, *The Dilbert Principle*, Boxtree, 1996

Aronson, Elliot, *The Social Animal*, W.H. Freeman, 1972

Barnes, JA, *Pack of Lies*, Cambridge University Press, 1994

Bridges, William, *Jobshift*, Nicholas Brealey, 1995

Collins, James and Porras, Jerry, *Built to Last*, HarperBusiness, 1994

Covey, Stephen, *The Seven Habits of Highly Effective People*, Simon & Schuster, 1992

Covey, Stephen, *First Things First*, Simon & Schuster, 1994

Davis, Stan and Botkin, Jim, *The Monster Under the Bed*, Touchstone, 1995

Dawson, Roger, *Make the Right Decision Every Time*, Nicholas Brealey, 1994

Drucker, Peter, *Managing the Non-Profit Organisation*, Butterworth Heinemann, 1990

Egan, Gerry, *The Skilled Helper*, Brooks/Cole, 1986

Fisher, Roger and Ury, William, *Getting to Yes*, Hutchinson, 1981

Fombrun, Charles J, *Reputation*, Harvard Business School Press, 1996

Fukuyama, Francis, *Trust*, Hamish Hamilton, 1995

Gardner, Howard, *Leading Minds*, HarperCollins, 1996

Hampden-Turner, Charles and Trompenaars, Fons, *The Seven Cultures of Capitalism*, Doubleday, 1993

Harvey-Jones, John, *Making It Happen*, Collins, 1988

Hope, Tony and Hope, Jeremy, *Transforming the Bottom Line*, Nicholas Brealey, 1995

Jampolsky, Lee, *The Art of Trust*, Celestial Arts, 1994

Katzenbach, Jon R and Smith, Douglas K, *The Wisdom of Teams*, Harvard Business School Press, 1993

Kennedy, Gavin, *Everything is Negotiable*, Arrow, 1984

Kleiner, Art, *The Age of Heretics*, Nicholas Brealey, 1996

Koch, Richard, *The Successful Boss's First 100 Days*, Pitman, 1994

Kouzes, James M and Posner, Barry Z, *Credibility*, Jossey-Bass, 1993

Kramer, Roderick M and Tyler, Tom R, *Trust in Organizations*, Sage, 1996

Leigh, Andrew and Maynard, Michael, *Leading Your Team*, Nicholas Brealey, 1995

Larkin, TJ and Larkin, Sandar, *Winning Employee Support for New Business Goals*, McGraw-Hill 1994

Maclean, Norman, *Young Men and Fire*, University of Chicago Press, 1992

Mant, Alistair, *Leaders We Deserve*, Martin Robertson, 1983

Manz, Charles C and Sims, Henry P, *Business Without Bosses*, John Wiley, 1993

McRae, Hamish, *The World in 2020*, HarperCollins, 1994

Milgram, Stanley, *Obedience to Authority*, Tavistock, 1974

Morgan, Gareth, *Images of Organization*, Sage, 1986

Nash, Laura, *Good Intentions Aside*, Harvard Business School Press, 1990

Packard, David, *The HP Way*, HarperCollins, 1995

Pearson, Gordon, *Integrity in Organizations*, McGraw-Hill, 1995

Peters, Tom, *Thriving on Chaos*, Macmillan, 1987

Peters, Tom, *Liberation Management*, Macmillan, 1992

Pfeffer, Jeffrey, *Managing with Power*, Harvard Business School Press, 1992

Rees, Goronwy, *St Michael: A History of Marks and Spencer*, Pan, 1969

Reichheld, Frederick F, *The Loyalty Effect*, Harvard Business School Press, 1996

Reynolds, Larry, *Beyond Total Quality Management*, Sheldon, 1994

Ryan, Kathleen and Oestreich, Daniel, *Driving Fear Out of the Workplace*, Jossey-Bass,1991

Sampson, Anthony, *Company Man*, HarperCollins, 1995

Schultz, Howard and Yang, Doris Jones, *Pour Your Heart into It*, Hyperion, 1997

Schuster, John and Carpenter, Jill, *The Power of Open Book Management*, John Wiley, 1996

Semler, Ricardo, *Maverick*, Century, 1993

Senge, Peter, *The Fifth Discipline*, Century, 1990

Shaw, Robert Bruce, *Trust in the Balance*, Jossey-Bass, 1997

Spector, Robert and McCarthy, Patrick, *The Nordstrom Way*, John Wiley, 1995

Spence, Gerry, *How to Argue and Win Every Time*, Sidgwick & Jackson, 1996

Stack, Jack, *The Great Game of Business*, Currency Doubleday, 1992

Taylor, Jim and Wacker, Watts, *The 500 Year Delta*, HarperBusiness, 1997

Wheeler, David and Sillanpää, Maria, *The Stakeholder Corporation*, Pitman, 1997

Whitney, John O, *The Trust Factor*, McGraw-Hill, 1993

Zeithaml, Valerie, Parasuraman, A and Berry, Leonard, *Delivering Quality Service*, Free Press, 1990

Index

Larry Reynolds can be contacted at:

Northern Consultancy
Meadowfield
Oxenhope
West Yorkshire
BD22 9JD

Tel: +44 (0)1535 645519
Fax: +44 (0)1535 645453
E-mail: northern@oxenhope.demon.co.uk